Velma Tour

GALÁPAGOS TRAVEL GUIDE

A Pocket Guide to Exploring Galápagos, Discover its Amazing Culture and History With 7-Days Itinerary Perfect for a First Timer

Copyright © 2023 Velma Tours

All Right Reserved

No part of this publication may be reproduced, distributed, or transmitted in any form or by any means, including photocopying, recording, or other electronic or mechanical methods, without the prior written permission of the author, except in the case of brief quotations embodied in critical reviews and specific other noncommercial uses permitted by copyright law.

This publication is protected by copyright law and international treaties. Unauthorized reproduction or distribution of this publication, or any portion of it, may result in severe civil and criminal penalties and will be prosecuted to the maximum extent possible under the law.

Every effort has been made to ensure that the contents of this publication are accurate and up-to-date. However, the author makes no warranties or representations, express or implied, regarding the information's completeness, accuracy, or reliability.

The views and opinions expressed in this publication are those of the author and do not necessarily reflect any agency or organization's official policy or position.

Table of Contents

Table of Contents 3
Introduction 6
Welcome to Galápagos 10
10 Interesting Reasons for Visiting Galápagos 18
15 Things You Should Know Before Visiting Galápagos 24
What to do and What Not to do in Galápagos 32
Do I Need a Visa to Visit Galápagos? 42
Visa Entry Requirement for Galápagos 48
List of Countries Whose Citizens are not Required to Get a Visa
.... 56
List of Countries Whose Citizens Need a Visa 64
Visa for Airport Transit 72
The Easiest Way to Purchase ticket and travel passes 80
Documents Needed 86
7 Days in Galápagos - A Complete One-Week Itinerary Guide .. 94
Getting Around Galápagos 102
   A Public Transportation Guide for First Timer 102
The Best Time to Visit for Honeymoon 108
The Best Time to Visit for Backpackers 114
The Best Time to Visit for Different Travelers 120
Seasons in Galápagos 124
A Month-to-Month Guide to Visiting Galápagos 132
Essentials Packs for Galápagos 150

3

The Most Necessary Items 156
Is Galápagos safe in the night? 162
Is it safe to Visit Galápagos? 166
Is Galápagos good for International Students? 172
Tips and Tricks for Staying Safe in Galápagos 178
Is it safe for Solo Female to Travel to Galápagos 184
Scams in Galápagos 190
What to do if in case of Emergency 194
Travel Protection Insurance 200
Where to Stay in Galápagos? 208
Resources for Solo Travelers 216
15 Best Place to Stay in Galápagos for Affordable Price 222
15 Best Luxuries Hotel to Stay in Galápagos 232
10 Most Delicious Food You Should Try in Galápagos 242
Conclusion 248

This page was left blank intentionally

Introduction

Once upon a time, in the enchanting archipelago of the Galápagos Islands, I embarked on an extraordinary adventure that would forever be etched in my memory. From the moment I set foot on the pristine shores, I was captivated by the breathtaking beauty and unique wildlife that inhabited this remote paradise.

My journey began on the island of Santa Cruz, where I stayed in a charming eco-lodge nestled amidst lush vegetation. The lodge blended seamlessly with its natural surroundings, offering a peaceful retreat after exhilarating days of exploration. Each morning, I awoke to the melodious chorus of birds, their vibrant songs welcoming me to a new day of discovery.

Eager to immerse myself in the wonders of the Galápagos, I set out on a guided tour to explore the nearby islands. One sunny morning, I found myself aboard a small boat, cruising through turquoise waters alongside a group of fellow adventurers. The air was filled with excitement as we anticipated the marvels that awaited us.

Our first stop was North Seymour Island, known for its magnificent frigatebirds and blue-footed boobies. As we approached the island's rocky shore, I marveled at the sight of these iconic birds, displaying their vibrant plumage and engaging in their captivating courtship rituals. It was a scene straight out of a nature documentary, but experiencing it firsthand was simply awe-inspiring.

From North Seymour, our journey took us to Bartolomé Island, famous for its lunar-like landscapes and breathtaking vistas. As we hiked to the island's summit, our guide shared fascinating insights into the volcanic formation of the Galápagos. At the top, we were rewarded with a panoramic view that took our breath away. The turquoise waters contrasted beautifully with the volcanic rocks, and the iconic Pinnacle Rock stood proudly in the distance. It was a picture-perfect moment that I wished would last forever.

The highlight of my Galápagos adventure came during an excursion to Española Island. Known as the "Island of Sea

Lions," it promised an up-close encounter with these playful creatures. As we approached the shore, the sight of sea lions basking lazily in the sun greeted us. The warm sand beneath my feet and the gentle sea breeze created a sense of tranquility that enveloped the island.

But it was the underwater world that truly stole my heart. Equipped with a snorkel and mask, I submerged into the crystal-clear waters, entering a world teeming with marine life. Colorful fish darted through the coral reefs, while graceful sea turtles glided effortlessly, their movements a mesmerizing ballet. Suddenly, a group of sea lions appeared, their agile bodies swirling around me. Curiosity sparked in their eyes as they effortlessly performed acrobatic maneuvers, inviting me to play. I couldn't resist the invitation and joined in their aquatic dance, laughing with pure joy as we swam together. It was a surreal moment of connection with nature that touched my soul.

Throughout my stay, I was humbled by the dedication of the local guides and their commitment to preserving the Galápagos' delicate ecosystem. They instilled in me a deep appreciation for the importance of responsible tourism and the need to protect this unique natural wonder for generations to come.

As the sun set on my final day in the Galápagos Islands, I found myself reflecting on the memories I had made. It was not just the incredible wildlife or stunning landscapes that had left an indelible mark, but the sense of harmony and serenity I had discovered amidst these remote islands.

The Galápagos had taught me that nature, when left undisturbed, can flourish in its purest form. It had awakened a sense of wonder within me, reminding me of the intricate web of life that we are all a part of. And as I bid farewell to this extraordinary archipelago, I carried with me a newfound respect for the natural world and a promise to tread lightly wherever my travels may take me.

The Galápagos Islands had transformed me, not just as a visitor, but as a guardian of our planet. The memories I had forged there would forever remind me of the beauty that exists when humans and nature coexist in harmony—a lesson I would cherish for a lifetime.

Welcome to Galápagos

A visit to the Galápagos Islands is an immersive experience that will leave an indelible mark on your soul. From the awe-inspiring encounters with wildlife to the breathtaking landscapes and the commitment to conservation, the Galápagos offers a truly unique and transformative journey.

Nestled in the Pacific Ocean, approximately 600 miles off the coast of Ecuador, lies a remote archipelago known as the Galápagos Islands. Stepping foot on these enchanting islands is like entering a different world—one where nature reigns supreme and wildlife roams freely. Welcome to the Galápagos, a place that has captured the hearts of explorers, scientists, and nature enthusiasts for centuries.

A Natural Laboratory

The Galápagos Islands are often referred to as a "living laboratory" due to their remarkable biodiversity and unique ecosystems. The archipelago is made up of 18 main islands, each with its own distinct characteristics and endemic species. The islands owe their rich biodiversity to their volcanic origins and their isolated location, which allowed for the evolution of distinct species over millions of years.

Upon arrival, visitors are greeted by a pristine and untouched environment, where human impact has been carefully managed to preserve the delicate balance of the ecosystem. The Galápagos National Park, established in 1959, covers over 97% of the land area, ensuring the protection of the islands' flora and fauna.

Wildlife Encounters

One of the main draws of the Galápagos Islands is the incredible wildlife that call this place home. Charles Darwin's visit to the archipelago in 1835 played a pivotal role in shaping his theory of evolution, as he observed the unique adaptations of the islands' inhabitants. Today, visitors have the opportunity to witness firsthand the wonders of natural selection and witness species found nowhere else on Earth.

As you explore the islands, you will encounter iconic wildlife such as the Galápagos giant tortoises, marine and land iguanas, and a variety of bird species. The blue-footed booby, with its vibrant blue feet, is a particular favorite among visitors. Watching these comical birds perform their elaborate courtship dance is a sight that will remain etched in your memory.

Another highlight is the Galápagos sea lions. These playful and curious creatures can be found lounging on the beaches or gracefully swimming through the crystal-clear waters. Snorkeling or diving alongside them is an incredible experience, as they showcase their agility and interact with visitors in their natural habitat.

Exploring the Islands

To truly appreciate the Galápagos Islands, it is best to explore multiple islands during your visit. There are two main ways to do this: by embarking on a cruise or by staying on one of the inhabited islands and taking day trips to nearby sites.

Cruising the archipelago offers a unique opportunity to visit more remote islands and allows for greater flexibility in terms of the sites you can explore. It is important to choose a reputable cruise operator that follows strict guidelines to minimize environmental impact. These cruises typically offer expert naturalist guides who provide valuable insights into the islands' wildlife and ecosystems.

Alternatively, staying on one of the inhabited islands, such as Santa Cruz or San Cristóbal, provides a chance to experience the local culture and enjoy the laid-back island lifestyle. From there, you can take day trips to nearby islands, visiting sites of interest and encountering wildlife along the way. Many tour operators offer guided excursions, ensuring a memorable and educational experience.

Conservation Efforts

Preserving the delicate balance of the Galápagos ecosystem is of paramount importance. The Galápagos National Park and the Charles Darwin Foundation work tirelessly to protect the islands' natural heritage. Strict regulations and guidelines are in place to ensure that visitors minimize their impact on the environment.

As a visitor, it is essential to adhere to these guidelines and respect the wildlife and their habitats. Keeping a safe distance from animals, not disturbing nesting or breeding areas, and avoiding littering are some of the ways you can contribute to the preservation of this unique environment. By following these responsible tourism practices, you become a partner in conservation, ensuring that future generations can continue to enjoy the wonders of the Galápagos.

Exploring the Underwater World

The Galápagos Islands are not only a haven for terrestrial wildlife but also offer exceptional opportunities for underwater exploration. The archipelago is renowned for its thriving marine ecosystem, attracting divers and snorkelers from around the world.

The nutrient-rich waters surrounding the islands support a diverse array of marine life. Schools of colorful tropical fish, sea turtles, rays, and even sharks can be spotted while snorkeling or diving. The fearless nature of the Galápagos wildlife extends beneath the waves, allowing for unforgettable encounters with marine species.

To ensure the preservation of the marine environment, certain areas are designated as marine reserves, where fishing and other activities are strictly regulated. Snorkeling and diving operators adhere to responsible practices, ensuring that visitors can enjoy the underwater world while minimizing disturbance to the marine life.

Cultural Experiences

While the Galápagos Islands are primarily known for their natural wonders, they also offer glimpses into the human history and culture of the archipelago. A visit to the inhabited islands provides an opportunity to interact with the local communities, learn about their way of life, and sample the unique Galápagos cuisine.

The Galápagos Islands have a rich human history, with early settlers arriving as early as the 1800s. Today, you can visit towns and villages, such as Puerto Ayora on Santa Cruz Island or Puerto Baquerizo Moreno on San Cristóbal Island, where you can explore local markets, shops, and restaurants.

Indigenous communities, such as the Kichwa people on Floreana Island, offer insights into their traditions and cultural practices. These encounters provide a deeper appreciation of the human connection to the islands and the importance of preserving both the natural and cultural heritage.

This page was left blank intentionally

10 Interesting Reasons for Visiting Galápagos

This pristine archipelago is renowned for its unique biodiversity, stunning landscapes, and the inspiration it provided to Charles Darwin's theory of evolution. If you're considering a trip to this extraordinary destination, here are ten (10) interesting reasons that will surely convince you to visit the Galápagos Islands.

1. Unparalleled Wildlife Encounters

One of the top reasons to visit the Galápagos Islands is the incredible wildlife encounters. The islands are home to a remarkable array of species, many of which are found nowhere else on Earth. From the iconic Galápagos giant tortoises to marine and land iguanas, blue-footed boobies, and Darwin's finches, the archipelago offers a unique opportunity to witness the wonders of natural selection up close.

2. The Birthplace of Evolutionary Theory

The Galápagos Islands hold historical significance as the birthplace of Charles Darwin's theory of evolution. It was during his visit to the archipelago in 1835 that Darwin observed the distinct adaptations of the island's wildlife, leading him to formulate his groundbreaking ideas. A visit to the Galápagos allows you to follow in Darwin's footsteps and gain a deeper understanding of the evolutionary processes that have shaped life on our planet.

3. Pristine and Protected Ecosystems

The Galápagos Islands boast pristine and protected ecosystems that have remained largely untouched by human activity. Over 97% of the land area is designated as a national park, ensuring the preservation of the islands' unique flora and fauna. Witnessing these untouched habitats is a humbling experience that allows for a deep appreciation of the delicate balance of nature.

4. Spectacular Landscapes

Beyond its rich wildlife, the Galápagos Islands showcase breathtaking landscapes that are a sight to behold. Volcanic craters, rugged coastlines, pristine beaches, and dramatic cliffs create a diverse and captivating environment. Whether you're hiking through volcanic terrains or enjoying panoramic views from atop a viewpoint, the landscapes of the Galápagos will leave you in awe.

5. Unspoiled Beaches and Crystal-Clear Waters

The Galápagos Islands are renowned for their unspoiled and idyllic beaches. These pristine stretches of sand offer the perfect spot to relax, soak up the sun, and enjoy the tranquil surroundings. The crystal-clear waters surrounding the islands are a paradise for snorkelers and divers, with vibrant coral reefs and an abundance of marine life to explore.

6. Extraordinary Snorkeling and Diving

The Galápagos Islands are a world-class snorkeling and diving destination. The nutrient-rich waters attract an incredible variety of marine species, including sea turtles, sea lions, rays, sharks, and countless colorful fish. Snorkelers and divers can explore vibrant coral reefs, underwater volcanic formations, and underwater caves, immersing themselves in a thriving marine ecosystem like no other.

7. Unique Photography Opportunities

For photography enthusiasts, the Galápagos Islands offer endless opportunities to capture stunning images. The charismatic wildlife, dramatic landscapes, and vibrant underwater scenes provide a wealth of subjects to capture through the lens. From close-up shots of a blue-footed booby to breathtaking sunsets over the ocean, every moment is a photo-worthy experience.

8. Cultural Experiences

While the Galápagos Islands are primarily known for their natural wonders, they also offer cultural experiences that add depth to your visit. Interacting with the local communities, learning about their way of life, and sampling traditional Galápagos cuisine provide a glimpse into the human history and cultural heritage of the archipelago. Exploring towns and villages allows you to connect with the islanders and gain insights into their traditions.

9. Educational and Scientific Significance

The Galápagos Islands hold immense educational and scientific significance. The unique ecosystems and endemic species provide a living laboratory for scientists and researchers studying various fields, including evolutionary biology, ecology, and conservation. Many organizations and research institutions conduct ongoing studies in the Galápagos, making it a hub for scientific discovery and education.

10. Responsible Tourism and Conservation Efforts

Visiting the Galápagos Islands offers an opportunity to engage in responsible tourism and contribute to conservation efforts. Strict regulations and guidelines are in place to protect the fragile ecosystem, and visitors are encouraged to follow responsible practices such as respecting wildlife, minimizing waste, and supporting local conservation initiatives. By visiting the Galápagos, you become a partner in the ongoing conservation of this natural treasure.

15 Things You Should Know Before Visiting Galápagos

Before you embark on your journey to this remarkable archipelago, here are 15 things you should know to make the most of your Galápagos adventure.

1. Protected National Park

The Galápagos Islands are designated as a national park, covering over 97% of the land area. This status ensures the preservation of the islands' delicate ecosystems and biodiversity. It also means that there are strict regulations in place to protect the environment and wildlife, so it's important to follow the guidelines set by the Galápagos National Park authorities.

2. Unique Wildlife

The Galápagos Islands are famous for their incredible wildlife. Many species found in the archipelago are endemic, meaning they are found nowhere else on Earth. From the iconic Galápagos giant tortoises to marine and land iguanas, sea lions, and a variety of bird species, the islands offer unparalleled opportunities for wildlife encounters and observation.

3. Natural Selection and Evolution

The Galápagos Islands played a pivotal role in shaping Charles Darwin's theory of evolution. During his visit in 1835, Darwin observed unique adaptations among the island's wildlife, leading to his groundbreaking ideas on natural selection. A visit to the Galápagos allows you to witness firsthand the principles of evolution and appreciate the diverse and specialized species that inhabit the islands.

4. Strict Visitor Guidelines

To preserve the fragile ecosystem of the Galápagos Islands, strict visitor guidelines are in place. These guidelines include maintaining a safe distance from wildlife, not touching or feeding the animals, and staying on designated paths and trails. Following these guidelines is essential to ensure the well-being of the wildlife and the long-term conservation of the islands.

5. Local Naturalist Guides

Exploring the Galápagos Islands is best done with the assistance of a local naturalist guide. These guides are highly knowledgeable about the islands' flora, fauna, and ecosystems, and provide valuable insights during your excursions. They also ensure that visitors adhere to the guidelines and make the most of their Galápagos experience.

6. Diverse Islands with Unique Characteristics

The Galápagos Islands consist of 18 main islands, each with its own distinct characteristics and ecosystems. From the volcanic landscapes of Isabela and Fernandina to the lush highlands of Santa Cruz and the seabird colonies of Española, every island offers a unique experience. Consider visiting multiple islands to appreciate the diversity of the archipelago.

7. Best Time to Visit

The Galápagos Islands can be visited year-round, as they have a mild and pleasant climate. However, the best time to visit depends on your preferences. The warm season from December to May offers calm seas, lush vegetation, and excellent diving conditions. The cool season from June to November is characterized by cooler temperatures, more active wildlife, and the presence of migratory species.

8. Getting to the Galápagos

To reach the Galápagos Islands, you must first fly to either Quito or Guayaquil in Ecuador. From there, you can take a domestic flight to the main airport on either Baltra Island or San Cristóbal Island. It's important to book your flights well in advance, as the number of visitors to the islands is regulated to minimize environmental impact.

9. Pack Accordingly

When packing for the Galápagos Islands, it's important to consider the activities you'll be engaging in and the varying weather conditions. Essentials include lightweight and breathable clothing, sturdy walking shoes or hiking boots, a hat, sunscreen, insect repellent, a reusable water bottle, and a waterproof bag for your camera and other valuables.

Don't forget your swimwear, snorkeling gear, and a lightweight waterproof jacket.

10. Sustainable Travel Practices

Sustainable travel practices are crucial in the Galápagos Islands to preserve the fragile environment. Follow the principles of responsible tourism, such as reducing waste, using biodegradable products, and avoiding single-use plastics. Respect the natural surroundings, avoid disturbing wildlife, and leave no trace of your presence.

11. Snorkeling and Diving Opportunities

The Galápagos Islands offer exceptional snorkeling and diving opportunities. The crystal-clear waters are teeming with marine life, including sea turtles, sea lions, rays, sharks, and colorful tropical fish. Consider bringing your own snorkeling gear for a more comfortable and personalized experience. If you're a certified diver, explore the underwater wonders with the guidance of experienced dive operators.

12. Extra Costs and Fees

When planning your Galápagos trip, be aware that there are additional costs and fees involved. These include the Galápagos National Park entry fee, the Ingala Transit Control Card fee, and the cost of transportation between islands. Budget accordingly to ensure you have a seamless and enjoyable experience.

13. Limited Infrastructure

The Galápagos Islands have limited infrastructure, particularly on the smaller, uninhabited islands. Facilities such as hotels, restaurants, and shops are concentrated in the populated islands like Santa Cruz and San Cristóbal. It's essential to book accommodations and make necessary arrangements in advance to ensure a comfortable stay.

14. Local Community Interaction

Interacting with the local communities in the Galápagos Islands offers a deeper understanding of the islands' culture and way of life. Visit the towns and villages, explore local markets, and support local businesses and artisans. Engaging with the locals can enrich your experience and contribute to the sustainability of the islands' economy.

15. Conservation and Responsible Tourism

The Galápagos Islands are a living laboratory for conservation and scientific research. By visiting the islands, you become a participant in ongoing conservation efforts. Support local conservation initiatives, respect the guidelines, and spread awareness about the importance of preserving the islands' unique ecosystems and wildlife.

This page was left blank intentionally

What to do and What Not to do in Galápagos

As a highly protected and fragile ecosystem, it's important to be aware of the dos and don'ts when visiting the Galápagos. In this chapter, I will provide comprehensive information on what to do and what not to do to ensure a responsible and enjoyable trip while preserving the islands' delicate environment and wildlife.

WHAT TO DO:

Follow the Guidelines of the Galápagos National Park

The Galápagos Islands are a protected national park, and strict guidelines are in place to ensure the preservation of the environment and wildlife. It's crucial to follow these guidelines, which include maintaining a safe distance from animals, not touching or feeding them, and staying on designated paths and trails. Listen to your naturalist guide and respect the regulations set by the Galápagos National Park authorities.

Engage with Local Naturalist Guides

Exploring the Galápagos Islands with the assistance of a local naturalist guide is highly recommended. These guides possess extensive knowledge about the islands' flora, fauna, and ecosystems. They will provide valuable insights, help you understand the unique characteristics of the wildlife, and ensure that you have a safe and informative experience.

Respect Wildlife and their Natural Habitat

Respecting the wildlife and their natural habitat is of utmost importance in the Galápagos Islands. Admire the animals from a safe distance, allowing them to behave naturally without disturbance. Avoid any attempts to touch, feed, or interfere with the wildlife. Remember, you are a guest in their home, and it's crucial to minimize your impact and ensure their well-being.

Practice Responsible Snorkeling and Diving

The Galápagos Islands offer exceptional opportunities for snorkeling and diving. When engaging in these activities, be mindful of the guidelines and practice responsible snorkeling and diving techniques. Avoid standing on or touching coral reefs, as they are delicate and take years to recover from any damage. Respect marine life and do not chase or harass them. Keep a safe distance to avoid accidental contact and maintain the natural balance of the underwater ecosystem.

Support Local Conservation Initiatives

The Galápagos Islands are at the forefront of conservation efforts. Show your support by visiting local conservation organizations, such as the Charles Darwin Research Station, and learn about their initiatives. Consider making a donation or getting involved in volunteer programs that contribute to the long-term sustainability of the islands. By supporting these initiatives, you become an active participant in the conservation of this unique ecosystem.

Explore Multiple Islands

The Galápagos Islands consist of numerous islands, each with its own distinct characteristics and wildlife. To fully appreciate the diversity of the archipelago, plan your visit to include multiple islands. Each island offers unique landscapes, wildlife encounters, and geological formations. Exploring different islands will provide a comprehensive understanding of the Galápagos' natural wonders.

Stay in Accredited Accommodations

When choosing accommodations in the Galápagos Islands, opt for establishments that are accredited by the Galápagos National Park Directorate. These accommodations follow sustainable practices and adhere to strict regulations to minimize their impact on the environment. Staying in accredited accommodations ensures that your visit supports responsible tourism and conservation efforts.

Experience Local Culture and Cuisine

While the wildlife and landscapes are the main attractions in the Galápagos, take the time to experience the local culture and cuisine. Visit the towns and villages, interact with the local communities, and appreciate their way of life. Sample traditional Galápagos cuisine, which often includes fresh seafood and local ingredients. Supporting local businesses and artisans contributes to the sustainable development of the islands.

Respect the Fragile Ecosystem

The Galápagos Islands are a fragile ecosystem, and even the smallest actions can have a significant impact. Minimize your waste by carrying a reusable water bottle and avoiding single-use plastics. Properly dispose of any trash in designated bins and avoid leaving any litter behind. Respect the fragility of the environment and leave no trace of your visit.

Educate Yourself and Spread Awareness

Before visiting the Galápagos Islands, educate yourself about the unique wildlife, geology, and conservation efforts. Learn about the history of the islands and the ongoing scientific research. Share your knowledge and experiences with others, both during and after your trip, to raise awareness about the importance of preserving the Galápagos for future generations.

WHAT NOT TO DO:

Do Not Approach or Disturb Wildlife

One of the most important rules in the Galápagos is to never approach or disturb the wildlife. Avoid getting too close to animals, as it can cause stress or alter their natural behaviors. Keep a safe distance and use binoculars or zoom lenses for a closer view. Do not attempt to touch, feed, or interact with the animals in any way.

Do Not Remove or Damage Natural Resources

The Galápagos Islands are home to unique plants, rocks, and other natural resources that contribute to the delicate ecosystem. It is strictly prohibited to remove or damage any natural resources, including rocks, shells, or plants. Respect the islands' biodiversity and leave everything as you found it.

Do Not Bring Invasive Species

To protect the native species and ecosystems of the Galápagos, it is crucial not to introduce any invasive species. Before arriving, thoroughly inspect your belongings, including footwear and camping gear, to remove any seeds, insects, or animals that could potentially disrupt the delicate balance of the islands' ecosystem.

Do Not Feed Wildlife

Feeding wildlife in the Galápagos is strictly prohibited. It disrupts natural feeding patterns and can lead to dependency on human food, which is detrimental to the animals' health. Avoid any temptation to feed animals, whether intentionally or unintentionally, and do not leave any food scraps or waste behind.

Do Not Use Flash Photography

Using flash photography is not allowed in the Galápagos Islands, particularly when photographing wildlife. The sudden burst of light can startle or stress the animals, and it may interfere with their natural behaviors. Instead, adjust your camera settings to capture natural lighting conditions and respect the well-being of the wildlife.

Do Not Stray from Designated Paths and Trails

To protect the fragile ecosystems of the Galápagos, it is essential to stay on designated paths and trails. Straying from these designated areas can cause damage to vegetation, disturb nesting sites, or trample delicate organisms. Always follow your guide's instructions and respect the signs and markers indicating the permitted routes.

Do Not Buy Souvenirs Made from Wildlife

When purchasing souvenirs in the Galápagos, be cautious of items made from wildlife, including shells, corals, or products derived from endangered species. Buying such items contributes to the illegal trade and threatens the survival of these species. Choose souvenirs that support local artisans or showcase the natural beauty of the islands without harming the environment.

Do Not Use Non-Biodegradable Products

To minimize your environmental impact, avoid using non-biodegradable products during your visit to the Galápagos.

This includes items such as single-use plastics, styrofoam, and aerosol cans. Instead, opt for eco-friendly alternatives, such as reusable water bottles, cloth bags, and biodegradable toiletries.

Do Not Ignore Safety Briefings and Instructions

During your visit to the Galápagos, you may participate in various activities, such as boat tours, snorkeling, or hiking. It is important to pay attention to safety briefings and instructions provided by your naturalist guide or activity operators. Follow their guidance to ensure your safety and the well-being of the wildlife and environment.

Do Not Support Unauthorized Guides or Operators

To ensure a responsible and ethical experience in the Galápagos, only engage with authorized guides and operators. These individuals and companies adhere to the necessary regulations and guidelines to protect the islands' natural resources. Supporting unauthorized guides or operators may contribute to unsustainable practices or illegal activities.

This page was left blank intentionally

Do I Need a Visa to Visit Galápagos?

In this chapter, I will provide you with all the information you need to know about visa requirements for visiting the Galápagos Islands, ensuring a smooth and hassle-free travel experience.

Visa Exemption for Certain Nationalities

Ecuador, the country to which the Galápagos Islands belong, has a visa exemption policy for many nationalities. This means that citizens from certain countries do not require a visa to enter Ecuador or visit the Galápagos Islands for tourism purposes. The duration of the visa exemption may vary depending on the nationality and the purpose of the visit.

For example, citizens of the United States, Canada, the United Kingdom, Australia, and most European countries do not need a visa to enter Ecuador or the Galápagos Islands for tourist stays of up to 90 days. This allows visitors ample time to explore the islands and experience their wonders.

However, it's important to note that visa exemption policies are subject to change, and it's always a good idea to check with the nearest Ecuadorian embassy or consulate in your home country for the most up-to-date information regarding visa requirements.

Transit Control Card (TCT)

While a visa might not be required for entry into the Galápagos Islands, there is another important document that you must obtain: The Transit Control Card (TCT), also known as the Ingala Transit Card. The TCT is a mandatory document for all visitors traveling to the Galápagos Islands, regardless of their nationality.

The purpose of the TCT is to control the entry and exit of visitors to the Galápagos Islands, as well as to collect important data for conservation and tourism management purposes. The card is valid for a maximum of 60 days and must be obtained upon arrival at the Quito or Guayaquil airports, or at the Baltra or San Cristóbal airports in the Galápagos.

To obtain the TCT, you will need to present your passport, a completed immigration form, and pay a fee, which is currently around $20. The TCT must be kept with you at all times during your stay in the Galápagos and presented upon departure.

Visa Requirements for Non-Exempt Nationalities

If you are a citizen of a country that is not exempt from visa requirements, you will need to apply for an appropriate visa before traveling to Ecuador and the Galápagos Islands. The type of visa you will need will depend on the purpose and duration of your visit.

Ecuador offers various types of visas, including tourist visas, business visas, work visas, and more. It's essential to determine the most suitable visa category for your trip and initiate the visa application process well in advance to avoid any delays or complications.

Tourist visas generally allow visitors to stay in Ecuador and the Galápagos Islands for a specific period, usually up to 90 days. To apply for a tourist visa, you will typically need to submit a completed visa application form, a valid passport with at least six months of validity remaining, proof of travel arrangements (such as flight itineraries), proof of accommodation bookings, proof of sufficient funds to cover your stay, and a passport-sized photograph.

The visa application process may also require additional documentation, such as a cover letter explaining the purpose of your trip, a bank statement, and proof of travel insurance. It's important to check the specific requirements with the Ecuadorian embassy or consulate in your home country and allow sufficient time for the visa application to be processed.

Extensions and Long-Term Stays

If you wish to stay in the Galápagos Islands for a longer period beyond the allowed visa duration, you may be able to apply for an extension. Extensions are granted on a case-by-case basis and are subject to approval by the Ecuadorian immigration authorities.

To apply for a visa extension, you will need to visit the regional office of the Ministry of Foreign Affairs in either Puerto Ayora on Santa Cruz Island or Puerto Baquerizo Moreno on San Cristóbal Island. There, you will need to submit a formal request along with the necessary documentation, such as a valid passport, proof of sufficient funds, and a compelling reason for the extension.

It's important to note that visa extensions are not guaranteed, and it's advisable to plan your trip within the allowed visa duration to avoid any complications or overstays.

Traveling to Galápagos via Ecuador

If you are planning to visit the Galápagos Islands, it's likely that you will first arrive in mainland Ecuador before continuing to the archipelago. In this case, it's important to consider the visa requirements for Ecuador as well.

As mentioned earlier, Ecuador has a visa exemption policy for many nationalities, allowing stays of up to 90 days for tourism purposes. However, if you plan to spend an extended period in mainland Ecuador before or after your visit to the Galápagos Islands, you may need to apply for a separate visa to cover your entire stay in the country.

Again, it's crucial to check the specific visa requirements for Ecuador with the nearest embassy or consulate in your home country to ensure compliance with the immigration regulations.

Visa Entry Requirement for Galápagos

Visiting the Galápagos Islands is a dream for many nature enthusiasts and adventure seekers. Understanding the visa entry requirements is crucial to ensure a smooth and hassle-free travel experience.

If you are a citizen of a country that enjoys visa exemption for Ecuador, you can visit the Galápagos Islands for tourism purposes without needing a visa. However, all visitors, regardless of their nationality, must obtain the Transit Control Card (TCT) upon arrival.

Ecuador's Visa Policy

The Galápagos Islands are part of Ecuador, and therefore, the visa entry requirements for the Galápagos are the same as those for mainland Ecuador. Ecuador has a relatively lenient visa policy, allowing visa-free entry for citizens of many countries for tourism purposes. However, it's crucial to check the specific visa regulations for your country of citizenship, as visa policies can change, and some exceptions may apply.

Visa Exemption for Tourism

Ecuador grants visa exemption to citizens of several countries for tourist stays of up to 90 days. This means that if you are a citizen of a country that falls under this visa exemption policy, you can visit the Galápagos Islands for tourism purposes without needing to obtain a visa in advance.

Countries that generally enjoy visa exemption for Ecuador include the United States, Canada, the United Kingdom, Australia, most European Union countries, and many others. However, it's important to note that the visa exemption policy can vary for different nationalities and the purpose of your visit.

The duration of the visa exemption is typically 90 days within a 12-month period. It's crucial to keep track of the number of days you spend in Ecuador, including both mainland Ecuador and the Galápagos Islands, to ensure that you comply with the visa regulations.

Transit Control Card (TCT)

While a visa might not be required for entry into the Galápagos Islands, there is an important document that all visitors must obtain upon arrival: the Transit Control Card (TCT), also known as the Ingala Transit Card. The TCT is a mandatory document for all visitors traveling to the Galápagos Islands, regardless of their nationality.

The purpose of the TCT is to control the entry and exit of visitors to the Galápagos Islands, as well as to collect important data for conservation and tourism management purposes. The card is valid for a maximum of 60 days and must be obtained upon arrival at the Quito or Guayaquil airports or at the Baltra or San Cristóbal airports in the Galápagos.

To obtain the TCT, you will need to present your passport, a completed immigration form, and pay a fee, which is currently around $20. The TCT must be kept with you at all times during your stay in the Galápagos and presented upon departure.

Visa Requirements for Non-Exempt Nationalities

If you are a citizen of a country that is not exempt from visa requirements, you will need to apply for an appropriate visa before traveling to Ecuador and the Galápagos Islands. The type of visa you need will depend on the purpose and duration of your visit.

Ecuador offers various types of visas, including tourist visas, business visas, work visas, and more. To visit the Galápagos Islands as a tourist, you will typically need to apply for a tourist visa, which allows for a specified period of stay in Ecuador and the Galápagos.

To apply for a tourist visa, you will generally need to submit the following documents:

- **Completed visa application form**: This form can be obtained from the nearest Ecuadorian embassy or consulate or downloaded from their official website.

- **Valid passport**: Your passport must have a minimum of six months' validity remaining from the date of entry into Ecuador.

- **Passport-sized photographs**: You will need to provide recent, color photographs that meet the specific requirements set by the embassy or consulate.

- **Proof of travel arrangements**: This can include round-trip flight itineraries or reservation confirmations.

- **Proof of accommodation**: You may need to provide hotel reservations or an invitation letter if you plan to stay with a host.

- **Financial documents:** Proof of sufficient funds to cover your stay in Ecuador, such as bank statements or traveler's checks.

- **Travel insurance**: Some visa applications may require proof of travel insurance coverage for the duration of your stay in Ecuador.

- **Additional documentation:** Depending on the embassy or consulate, you may be asked to provide additional supporting documents, such as a cover letter explaining the purpose of your trip, a detailed itinerary, or a criminal record clearance certificate.

It's important to note that visa application requirements may vary depending on the country you are applying from and the specific embassy or consulate you are dealing with. It is recommended to contact the nearest Ecuadorian embassy or consulate for the most accurate and up-to-date information regarding visa application requirements.

Visa Application Process

To apply for a visa, you will typically need to submit your visa application and supporting documents in person at the Ecuadorian embassy or consulate in your home country. Some embassies or consulates may allow visa applications by mail, but it's generally advisable to apply in person whenever possible.

During the application process, you may be required to pay a visa fee, which can vary depending on your nationality and the type of visa you are applying for. The fee is non-refundable, even if your visa application is not approved.

It's important to allow sufficient time for the visa application to be processed. Visa processing times can vary depending on the embassy or consulate and the time of year. It is recommended to apply for your visa well in advance of your planned travel dates to avoid any potential delays or complications.

Visa Extensions

If you wish to stay in the Galápagos Islands for a longer period beyond the allowed visa duration, you may be able to apply for a visa extension. Visa extensions are granted on a case-by-case basis and are subject to approval by the Ecuadorian immigration authorities.

To apply for a visa extension, you will need to visit the regional office of the Ministry of Foreign Affairs in either Puerto Ayora on Santa Cruz Island or Puerto Baquerizo Moreno on San Cristóbal Island. There, you will need to submit a formal request along with the necessary documentation, such as a valid passport, proof of sufficient funds, and a compelling reason for the extension.

It's important to note that visa extensions are not guaranteed, and it's advisable to plan your trip within the allowed visa duration to avoid any complications or overstays.

List of Countries Whose Citizens are not Required to Get a Visa

Knowing the visa requirements of a destination country is crucial for hassle-free travel planning. This comprehensive list highlights countries that allow visa exemption for citizens of various nations, facilitating easy and convenient travel.

It's important to remember that visa policies can change, and there may be specific conditions and limitations for visa-free entry, such as the purpose and duration of the visit. Therefore, it is always recommended to check with the respective embassy or consulate of the destination country or consult official government resources for the most accurate and up-to-date information regarding visa requirements.

Traveling to different countries is an exciting experience that allows us to explore new cultures, landscapes, and traditions. However, one of the essential aspects of international travel is understanding the visa requirements of the destination country. Some countries have agreements that exempt certain nationalities from obtaining a visa for short-term visits. In this chapter, I will provide you with a detailed list of countries whose citizens are not required to get a visa, making it easier for you to plan your travels with ease and confidence.

Before we delve into the list, it's important to note that visa policies can change over time, so it's always advisable to double-check with the respective embassy or consulate of the destination country to ensure the most up-to-date information.

United States

The United States, one of the most popular tourist destinations, allows citizens from several countries to travel visa-free under the Visa Waiver Program (VWP). The VWP allows citizens from eligible countries to visit the U.S. for tourism or business purposes for up to 90 days without obtaining a visa.

Canada

Similar to the United States, Canada also grants visa exemption to citizens from various countries. Under Canada's Electronic Travel Authorization (eTA) program, citizens from eligible countries can visit Canada for tourism, business, or transit purposes for up to six months without a visa.

United Kingdom

The United Kingdom offers visa exemption to citizens of many countries. Visitors from these countries can enter the UK for tourism, business, or transit purposes for up to six months without obtaining a visa. However, it's important to note that citizens from some countries may still need to obtain an entry clearance called an Electronic Visa Waiver (EVW) before traveling to the UK.

Australia

Australia has a visa exemption policy for citizens of several countries. Under the Electronic Travel Authority (ETA) system, eligible travelers can visit Australia for tourism, business, or visiting family and friends for up to three months without a visa. The ETA can be easily applied for online.

Schengen Area Countries

The Schengen Area, comprising 26 European countries, allows citizens of certain countries to travel within the area without a visa. These countries include Austria, Belgium, Czech Republic, Denmark, Estonia, Finland, France, Germany, Greece, Hungary, Iceland, Italy, Latvia, Liechtenstein, Lithuania, Luxembourg, Malta, Netherlands, Norway, Poland, Portugal, Slovakia, Slovenia, Spain, Sweden, and Switzerland. Travelers from visa-exempt countries can visit any Schengen country for up to 90 days within a 180-day period.

New Zealand

New Zealand offers visa exemption to citizens of many countries. Visitors from these countries can enter New Zealand for tourism, business, or transit purposes for up to three months without obtaining a visa.

Japan

Japan allows citizens from numerous countries to visit for tourism or business purposes without a visa for up to 90 days. The list of visa-exempt countries for Japan includes the United States, Canada, the United Kingdom, Australia, New Zealand, most European Union countries, and many others.

Singapore

Singapore has a visa exemption policy for citizens of several countries. Visitors from these countries can enter Singapore for tourism or business purposes for up to 30 days without a visa.

South Korea

South Korea offers visa exemption to citizens of many countries. Under the visa waiver program, travelers from these countries can enter South Korea for tourism or business purposes for a specified period without obtaining a visa.

Malaysia

Malaysia allows citizens from various countries to enter without a visa for tourism, business, or transit purposes for a specific duration. The visa exemption period can vary depending on the nationality.

Brazil

Brazil grants visa exemption to citizens of several countries for tourism or business purposes. The duration of visa-free stays can vary depending on the nationality.

Argentina

Argentina allows visa-free entry for citizens of many countries. Visitors from these countries can travel to Argentina for tourism or business purposes for a specified period without obtaining a visa.

Chile

Chile offers visa exemption to citizens of numerous countries. Visitors from these countries can enter Chile for tourism or business purposes without obtaining a visa, subject to certain conditions and duration limitations.

South Africa

South Africa has a visa exemption policy for citizens of several countries. Visitors from these countries can enter South Africa for tourism or business purposes without a visa for a specified period.

United Arab Emirates

The United Arab Emirates (UAE) allows citizens of many countries to enter without a visa for tourism or business purposes. The visa exemption period can vary depending on the nationality.

This page was left blank intentionally

List of Countries Whose Citizens Need a Visa

International travel often requires obtaining a visa, which grants permission for entry into a foreign country. Visa requirements vary from country to country, and it is important for travelers to be aware of these requirements in order to plan their trips effectively. In this chapter, I will provide a detailed list of countries whose citizens need a visa to enter, helping you navigate the visa application process and ensuring a smooth travel experience.

Before we delve into the list, it is crucial to note that visa policies can change over time, and it is advisable to check with the respective embassy or consulate of the destination country for the most up-to-date and accurate information.

China

China requires citizens of most countries to obtain a visa before entering the country. The type of visa required depends on the purpose of the visit, such as tourism, business, or work. Travelers to China typically need to apply for a visa at the nearest Chinese embassy or consulate in their home country.

Russia

Citizens of many countries are required to obtain a visa to visit Russia. The Russian visa application process involves submitting the necessary documents, such as a valid passport, visa application form, invitation letter, and supporting documents, to the Russian embassy or consulate in the traveler's home country.

India

India requires citizens of most countries to obtain a visa prior to travel. The Indian visa application process involves completing an online application, submitting the required documents, such as a valid passport, passport-sized photographs, and proof of travel arrangements, and attending an appointment at the nearest Indian embassy or consulate.

Brazil

Brazil requires citizens of many countries to obtain a visa before traveling. The visa application process for Brazil typically involves completing an online application form, submitting the required documents, such as a valid passport, proof of travel arrangements, and a visa fee, and attending an appointment at the nearest Brazilian embassy or consulate.

Australia

Australia generally requires citizens of most countries to obtain a visa before entering the country. The Australian visa application process involves applying online through the Department of Home Affairs website, submitting the required documents, such as a valid passport, proof of travel arrangements, and paying the visa fee.

Saudi Arabia

Saudi Arabia requires citizens of most countries to obtain a visa before visiting the country. In recent years, Saudi Arabia has introduced the eVisa system, allowing eligible travelers to apply for a visa online. The visa application process may also involve providing a letter of invitation, medical reports, and other supporting documents.

Vietnam

Vietnam typically requires citizens of most countries to obtain a visa prior to travel. The visa application process for Vietnam involves submitting an online application, paying the visa fee, and receiving an approval letter, which must be presented upon arrival at the designated entry points in Vietnam.

Egypt

Egypt requires citizens of many countries to obtain a visa before visiting. The visa application process for Egypt usually involves completing an online application form, providing the required documents, such as a valid passport, passport-sized photographs, and paying the visa fee. Some travelers may also be eligible for a visa on arrival.

Turkey

Turkey generally requires citizens of most countries to obtain a visa before traveling. The visa application process for Turkey involves applying online or at a Turkish embassy or consulate, submitting the required documents, such as a valid passport, proof of travel arrangements, and paying the visa fee.

Canada

Canada requires citizens of many countries to obtain a visa before entering the country. The Canadian visa application process involves completing an online application or submitting a paper application, providing the necessary documents, such as a valid passport, proof of travel arrangements, and attending a biometrics appointment if required.

United Arab Emirates

The United Arab Emirates (UAE) requires citizens of several countries to obtain a visa before visiting. The visa application process for the UAE typically involves applying online or through a sponsor, submitting the required documents, such as a valid passport, photographs, and paying the visa fee.

United States

The United States generally requires citizens of most countries to obtain a visa before entering the country. The visa application process for the U.S. involves completing the online nonimmigrant visa application, paying the visa fee, and scheduling an appointment at the nearest U.S. embassy or consulate for an interview.

South Africa

South Africa requires citizens of many countries to obtain a visa before traveling. The visa application process for South Africa involves submitting the required documents, such as a valid passport, completed visa application form, proof of travel arrangements, and paying the visa fee at the nearest South African embassy or consulate.

Argentina

Argentina requires citizens of many countries to obtain a visa before visiting. The visa application process for Argentina typically involves completing an online application, submitting the necessary documents, such as a valid passport, proof of travel arrangements, and paying the visa fee.

Egypt

Egypt requires citizens of many countries to obtain a visa before visiting. The visa application process for Egypt usually involves completing an online application form, providing the required documents, such as a valid passport, passport-sized photographs, and paying the visa fee. Some travelers may also be eligible for a visa on arrival.

This page was left blank intentionally

Visa for Airport Transit

Airport transit visas, also known as transit visas or A visas, are a type of visa required by certain travelers who are transiting through an airport in a country without actually entering that country's territory. These visas allow travelers to transit through the airport and continue their journey to their final destination. In this chapter, I will provide detailed information about airport transit visas, including the countries that require them, the application process, and other important considerations.

Before we proceed, it is important to note that visa regulations can change over time, and it is always advisable to check with the respective embassy or consulate of the transit country for the most up-to-date and accurate information.

What is an Airport Transit Visa?

An airport transit visa is a travel document that allows travelers to pass through the international transit area of an airport in a country without entering the country's territory. It is typically required when a traveler has a layover or connecting flight in a country where they would normally require a visa to enter.

The purpose of an airport transit visa is to ensure that travelers do not illegally enter the country during their transit. It is important to note that the requirements for an airport transit visa may vary from country to country, and not all countries require it for transit purposes.

Countries that Require Airport Transit Visas

The requirement for an airport transit visa depends on the country and the traveler's nationality. Some countries have a general policy of requiring transit visas for all travelers, while others have specific requirements based on the traveler's nationality and the length of the layover. Here are some examples of countries that require airport transit visas:

a. **United Kingdom**: The United Kingdom requires certain nationalities to obtain a Direct Airside Transit Visa (DATV) if they are transiting through a UK airport without entering the UK. The DATV allows travelers to stay in the international transit area of the airport for up to 24 hours.

b. **United States**: The United States requires certain nationalities to obtain a C-1 transit visa if they are transiting through a U.S. airport without entering the U.S. This visa allows travelers to stay in the international transit area of the airport for a limited period.

c. **Canada**: Canada requires certain nationalities to obtain a transit visa if they are transiting through a Canadian airport without entering Canada. The transit visa allows travelers to stay in the international transit area of the airport for a limited time.

d. **Schengen Area**: The Schengen Area, comprising 26 European countries, requires certain nationalities to obtain an airport transit visa (also known as an "A" visa) if they are transiting through a Schengen airport without entering any of the Schengen countries. The A visa allows travelers to stay in the international transit area of the airport for a limited period.

Application Process for Airport Transit Visa

The application process for an airport transit visa may vary depending on the country and the traveler's nationality. Generally, it involves the following steps:

a. **Determine the Requirement**: Check the visa requirement for airport transit in the country you will be transiting through. Visit the website of the embassy or consulate of the transit country or consult official government resources to find out if you need an airport transit visa.

b. **Gather Required Documents**: Once you determine the visa requirement, gather the necessary documents for the application. This typically includes a valid passport, proof of onward travel (such as flight tickets), and any additional documents required by the transit country.

c. **Complete the Application**: Fill out the visa application form accurately and completely. Provide all the requested information, including personal details, travel itinerary, and any other required information.

d. **Submit the Application**: Submit the completed visa application along with the required documents to the embassy or consulate of the transit country. This can typically be done in person or by mail, depending on the country.

e. **Pay the Visa Fee**: Pay the applicable visa fee. The fee amount may vary depending on the transit country and the traveler's nationality. Ensure that you have the correct payment method accepted by the embassy or consulate.

f. **Attend an Interview**: In some cases, an interview may be required as part of the visa application process. If an interview is scheduled, make sure to attend it on the specified date and time.

g. **Wait for Processing**: The processing time for an airport transit visa varies depending on the transit country and the embassy or consulate's workload. It is advisable to apply well in advance to allow sufficient time for processing.

h. **Collect the Visa**: Once the visa is approved, collect it from the embassy or consulate. Verify that all the details on the visa are correct before leaving the premises.

Important Considerations for Airport Transit Visa

When applying for an airport transit visa, there are a few important considerations to keep in mind:

a. **Validity**: Ensure that your passport is valid for at least six months beyond the date of your planned transit. Some countries may also require a certain number of blank pages in your passport for visa stamps.

b. **Duration of Stay**: An airport transit visa allows you to stay in the international transit area of the airport for a limited period. It does not allow you to leave the airport or enter the country. Make sure you have sufficient time between flights to complete your transit.

c. **Visa-Free Transit:** In some cases, certain nationalities may be exempt from obtaining an airport transit visa if they meet specific conditions. For example, some countries allow visa-free transit for short layovers or if the traveler holds a valid visa for their final destination.

d. **Additional Requirements**: Some countries may have additional requirements for an airport transit visa, such as proof of accommodation, travel insurance, or financial means to support yourself during the transit.

e. **Consult Official Sources**: Always refer to the official website of the embassy or consulate of the transit country for the most accurate and up-to-date information regarding the application process, required documents, and visa fees.

This page was left blank intentionally

The Easiest Way to Purchase ticket and travel passes

Purchasing tickets and travel passes has become increasingly convenient in today's digital age. Online booking platforms, mobile apps, travel agencies, self-service kiosks, and hotel services all provide different avenues for acquiring the necessary tickets and passes for your travel needs. Whether it's flights, trains, buses, or local attractions, these options offer simplicity, flexibility, and ease of use.

Traveling to new destinations often requires purchasing tickets and travel passes to access transportation services such as flights, trains, buses, or even local attractions. In today's digital age, various platforms and methods have made it easier than ever to acquire these tickets and passes conveniently. In this chapter, I will explore the easiest ways to purchase tickets and travel passes, ensuring a smooth and hassle-free travel experience.

Online Booking Platforms

One of the simplest and most convenient ways to purchase tickets and travel passes is through online booking platforms. These platforms provide a centralized hub where travelers can browse and book tickets for various modes of transportation and attractions. Some popular online booking platforms include:

a. **Airline Websites**: Most airlines have their own websites where travelers can search for flights, select their preferred options, and purchase tickets online. These websites often offer additional services such as seat selection and online check-in.

b. **Travel Aggregator Websites**: Travel aggregator websites gather information from multiple airlines, hotels, and transportation providers, allowing users to compare prices and book tickets and travel passes all in one place. Examples include Expedia, Kayak, and Skyscanner.

c. **Train and Bus Booking Websites**: Many countries have dedicated websites or apps for booking train and bus tickets. These platforms provide schedules, availability, and the option to purchase tickets online. Examples include Rail Europe for train travel in Europe and RedBus for bus travel in various countries.

d. **Attractions and Activities Websites**: For purchasing passes to local attractions or activities, websites such as Viator, GetYourGuide, and TripAdvisor offer a wide range of options. Travelers can browse through various experiences, read reviews, and book tickets in advance.

Mobile Apps

Mobile apps have revolutionized the way we travel, offering convenience and accessibility right at our fingertips. With travel-related apps, purchasing tickets and travel passes has become easier than ever. Here are some types of mobile apps that facilitate ticket and pass purchases:

a. **Airline Apps**: Most airlines have their own mobile apps, allowing travelers to search for flights, book tickets, manage reservations, and receive real-time updates about their journey. These apps often provide a seamless mobile check-in experience as well.

b. **Travel Aggregator Apps:** Similar to their web counterparts, travel aggregator apps such as Expedia, Kayak, and Skyscanner enable users to search and book flights, hotels, and rental cars, making it convenient to plan and purchase travel-related services.

c. **Public Transportation Apps**: Many cities and regions have their own public transportation apps that offer features like real-time schedules, route planning, and mobile ticketing. Examples include Citymapper, Moovit, and Transit App.

d. **Mobile Wallets:** Mobile wallet apps such as Apple Pay, Google Pay, and Samsung Pay allow users to store payment information securely and make contactless payments. Some transportation providers and attractions accept mobile payments, eliminating the need for physical tickets or passes.

Travel Agencies and Tour Operators

While online platforms and mobile apps have gained popularity, traditional travel agencies and tour operators still offer convenience and personalized assistance for purchasing tickets and travel passes. These professionals have in-depth knowledge and can provide valuable recommendations and guidance. Travelers can visit a local travel agency or contact tour operators specializing in specific destinations or types of travel.

Self-Service Kiosks

Self-service kiosks are commonly found at airports, train stations, and major transportation hubs. These kiosks allow travelers to purchase tickets, check-in for flights, and print boarding passes or travel passes. They provide a user-friendly interface where travelers can follow step-by-step instructions to complete their transactions independently.

Hotel Concierge and Front Desk

For local transportation options or attractions, hotel concierge and front desk services can be a valuable resource. They can provide information about nearby transportation options, assist in booking tickets, and even offer recommendations based on their local knowledge.

Documents Needed

When preparing for a trip, it is crucial to ensure you have all the necessary documents in order to travel smoothly and comply with immigration and security regulations. The specific documents required may vary depending on your destination, nationality, and purpose of travel. In this chapter, I will discuss the essential documents needed for travel, including identification documents, travel visas, passports, and additional documentation that may be required for specific circumstances.

Passport

A passport is the most important travel document that serves as proof of identity and citizenship. It allows you to travel internationally and provides access to foreign countries. When applying for a passport, ensure it is valid for at least six months beyond your planned return date, as many countries have this requirement. It is advisable to apply for a passport well in advance of your travel dates, as processing times may vary.

Visas

Visas are official documents issued by a country's embassy or consulate that grant you permission to enter and stay within that country for a specific period and purpose. The visa requirements depend on your nationality and the destination country. Some countries allow visa-free entry for certain nationalities, while others require a visa in advance or upon arrival. Research the visa requirements for your destination country and apply accordingly, allowing sufficient time for processing.

Travel Visa Waivers

Certain countries have implemented travel visa waiver programs, which allow eligible travelers to visit for a limited period without a visa. Examples include the Visa Waiver Program (VWP) for the United States and the Electronic Travel Authorization (ETA) for Canada. These programs typically require travelers to obtain an electronic authorization in advance of their trip. Check if your nationality qualifies for such visa waiver programs and follow the necessary procedures.

Electronic Travel Authorization (ETA)

An Electronic Travel Authorization (ETA) is a form of electronic authorization required by some countries for short-term visits. It is usually obtained online prior to travel and serves as an alternative to a traditional visa. Countries such as Australia, Sri Lanka, and India have implemented ETA systems. Ensure you apply for an ETA, if required, and receive approval before your departure.

Identification Documents

Aside from a passport, it is essential to carry additional identification documents for domestic and international travel. These may include:

a. **National Identity Card**: In some countries, a national identity card is a valid form of identification for both domestic and international travel. Ensure that your identity card is accepted for travel purposes and is not expired.

b. **Driver's License**: A driver's license can serve as an additional form of identification, especially for domestic travel or as supplementary identification alongside your passport.

c. **Student ID Card**: If you are a student traveling internationally, carrying a valid student identification card may entitle you to certain discounts and benefits at various attractions, accommodations, or transportation services.

d. **Medical ID Cards**: If you have specific medical conditions or allergies, carrying a medical ID card can provide important information to healthcare professionals in case of emergencies.

Travel Itinerary

Having a detailed travel itinerary is essential, especially when traveling internationally. It helps you stay organized and provides vital information about your trip. Your travel itinerary should include flight details, hotel reservations, contact information of accommodations and travel agents, and a comprehensive schedule of your activities. This document can serve as proof of your intended travel plans and can be requested by immigration officials or security personnel.

a. Proof of Accommodation

Most countries require visitors to provide proof of accommodation during their stay. This can be in the form of hotel reservations, a letter of invitation from a host, or a rental agreement if you are staying at a vacation rental. Ensure you have these documents readily available to present when requested.

b. Proof of Sufficient Funds

Immigration authorities may require you to provide proof of sufficient funds to cover your expenses during your stay. This can be in the form of bank statements, credit card statements, or traveler's checks. The required amount may vary depending on your destination and the duration of your visit. It is important to have these documents available, even if they are not explicitly requested.

c. Travel Insurance

While not mandatory in all countries, travel insurance is highly recommended to protect yourself from unexpected medical emergencies, trip cancellations, or lost luggage. It is advisable to carry a copy of your travel insurance policy or the contact information of your insurance provider. This will allow you to access necessary assistance and support during your trip.

d. Health and Vaccination Documents

Depending on your destination, you may be required to provide health-related documents, such as proof of vaccination or a yellow fever certificate. Some countries have specific entry requirements related to contagious diseases. Check the vaccination requirements for your destination well in advance and ensure you have the necessary documentation.

e. Consent Letters for Minors

If you are traveling with a minor child who is not accompanied by both parents, you may be required to provide a consent letter from the absent parent(s) granting permission for the child to travel. This helps prevent any potential legal issues or concerns related to child custody. Check the specific requirements of your destination country and prepare the necessary consent letters, if applicable.

Additional Documents for Specific Circumstances

Depending on your travel purpose or circumstances, additional documents may be required. These can include:

a. **Business Travel**: If you are traveling for business purposes, you may need to provide documents such as a letter of invitation, conference registrations, or proof of employment.

b. **Work Permits**: If you are planning to work abroad, you may require a work permit or visa specific to your employment.

c. **Study Abroad**: Students planning to study abroad should have their acceptance letter from the educational institution, proof of enrollment, and any necessary student visas.

d. **Specialized Activities**: Certain activities, such as volunteering, research, or attending cultural events, may require specific permits or letters of authorization. Research the requirements for your chosen activity and prepare the appropriate documents.

7 Days in Galápagos - A Complete One-Week Itinerary Guide

A week in the Galápagos Islands offers a diverse and enriching experience, allowing you to immerse yourself in the natural wonders of this unique destination. From encountering wildlife to exploring volcanic landscapes and relaxing on pristine beaches, each day of this itinerary brings new adventures and opportunities to connect with the incredible biodiversity of the Galápagos.

Remember to respect the fragile ecosystem and follow the guidelines set by the Galápagos National Park to ensure the preservation of this remarkable archipelago for future generations. In this comprehensive one-week itinerary guide, we will explore a suggested itinerary for spending 7 days in the Galápagos Islands, highlighting the best attractions and activities to make the most of your visit.

Day 1: Arrival in Baltra and Santa Cruz Island

Upon arrival at Baltra Airport, you will be greeted by your guide and transferred to the Itabaca Channel, where a ferry will take you to Santa Cruz Island. Once on the island, head to Puerto Ayora, the main town in the Galápagos, where you can check into your accommodation and freshen up.

In the afternoon, visit the Charles Darwin Research Station, a renowned scientific research center dedicated to the conservation of the Galápagos Islands. Here, you can learn about ongoing conservation efforts and see giant tortoises up close. Take a stroll through the station's informative exhibits and explore the surrounding grounds.

Day 2: Isabela Island - Sierra Negra Volcano and Tintoreras Islet

Take a boat from Santa Cruz to Isabela Island, the largest island in the Galápagos archipelago. Begin your day by embarking on a hike to Sierra Negra Volcano, one of the most active volcanoes in the Galápagos. Enjoy panoramic views of the volcanic landscape and the expansive caldera, which stretches over 6 miles in diameter.

Afterward, visit Tintoreras Islet, a small volcanic island teeming with wildlife. Take a guided tour around the islet, where you can spot marine iguanas, sea lions, penguins, and an array of bird species. Snorkel in the crystal-clear waters and observe the diverse underwater ecosystem, including colorful fish and perhaps even sharks.

Day 3: Floreana Island - Post Office Bay and Punta Cormorant

Head to Floreana Island, known for its intriguing history and pristine beaches. Start your day at Post Office Bay, where an 18th-century tradition of leaving and collecting mail in a wooden barrel still persists. Leave a postcard or letter for a future visitor, or try your luck at finding mail to deliver to its intended recipient.

Next, visit Punta Cormorant, a beautiful beach with contrasting sand colors. Take a walk along the trail to a lagoon frequented by flamingos, and continue to a pristine white sand beach known as Flour Beach. Enjoy snorkeling in the crystal-clear waters, where you can swim alongside sea turtles and playful sea lions.

Day 4: North Seymour Island and Santa Fe Island

Embark on a day trip to North Seymour Island, a small but vibrant island known for its abundant wildlife. Take a guided walk along the trails, where you can observe nesting frigatebirds, blue-footed boobies, and land iguanas. Marvel at the intricate courtship displays of the blue-footed boobies, a signature sight in the Galápagos.

In the afternoon, visit Santa Fe Island, home to a unique species of land iguana and a picturesque cove perfect for snorkeling. Dive into the water to swim with sea lions, tropical fish, and perhaps even spot a passing eagle ray or reef shark. Explore the island's rocky trails and marvel at the stunning landscapes.

Day 5: Bartolomé Island and Sullivan Bay

Embark on a day trip to Bartolomé Island, one of the most iconic destinations in the Galápagos. Climb to the summit of Bartolomé Hill, where you will be rewarded with breathtaking panoramic views of the surrounding islands and the famous Pinnacle Rock. This distinctive rock formation is a popular symbol of the Galápagos.

Afterward, head to Sullivan Bay, a site known for its stunning volcanic formations. Walk along the hardened lava flows and witness the unique geological features formed by past volcanic eruptions. The stark black lava fields offer a striking contrast against the turquoise waters of the bay.

Day 6: Española Island - Gardner Bay and Punta Suarez

Visit Española Island, known for its remarkable wildlife and pristine beaches. Begin your day at Gardner Bay, a beautiful sandy beach where sea lions bask in the sun. Take a leisurely walk along the shore, snorkel in the clear waters, or simply relax and soak up the natural beauty.

In the afternoon, head to Punta Suarez, a remarkable site for birdwatching. Witness the incredible mating rituals of blue-footed boobies, as well as the colorful displays of waved albatrosses. Keep an eye out for marine iguanas, sea lions, and Galápagos hawks as you explore the rugged trails and stunning cliffs.

Day 7: Santa Cruz Island - Tortuga Bay and Departure

Spend your last day exploring Santa Cruz Island. Begin by visiting Tortuga Bay, a stunning white sand beach known for its pristine waters and abundant marine life. Take a walk along the trail to Tortuga Bay, keeping an eye out for marine iguanas and various bird species. Enjoy swimming, snorkeling, or simply relaxing on the beach.

In the afternoon, take some time to explore Puerto Ayora's local markets and shops, where you can find unique souvenirs and local crafts. Bid farewell to the Galápagos as you head back to Baltra Airport for your departure, taking with you memories of an unforgettable week in this extraordinary archipelago.

Getting Around Galápagos

A Public Transportation Guide for First Timer

Navigating the Galápagos Islands' transportation system can be an exciting part of your adventure. Whether you choose to fly between islands, hop on a public boat, explore on foot, or join guided tours, each mode of transportation offers a unique experience and an opportunity to immerse yourself in the natural wonders of the archipelago. In this chapter, I will provide an overview of public transportation in the Galápagos, offering valuable insights and tips for first-time visitors.

A Public Transportation Guide for First Timers

a. Inter-Island Flights

Inter-island flights are a popular and convenient way to travel between the main islands of the Galápagos. The two primary airports in the archipelago are Seymour Airport on

Baltra Island and San Cristóbal Airport on San Cristóbal Island. Several airlines offer regular flights between these two airports, as well as to other islands like Isabela and Floreana. It's advisable to book your inter-island flights in advance to secure the best prices and availability.

b. Public Boats

Public boats, also known as "lanchas," are another common mode of transportation for inter-island travel. These boats operate on fixed schedules and connect the main islands. While public boats are a more budget-friendly option compared to flights, they often have limited capacity and may not offer as much comfort or convenience. It's important to check the schedules and make reservations in advance, especially during peak tourist seasons.

c. Private Boats and Yachts

For those seeking a more personalized and flexible experience, private boats and yachts are available for charter in the Galápagos. This option allows you to customize your itinerary and explore the islands at your own pace. Private boats and yachts can accommodate various group sizes and offer amenities like comfortable cabins, onboard meals, and guided tours. However, it's worth noting that private charters can be more expensive than other transportation options.

d. Taxis and Buses on Santa Cruz Island

Santa Cruz Island, the most populated island in the Galápagos, has a reliable taxi and bus service that makes getting around the island convenient. Taxis are readily available in the main town of Puerto Ayora and can be hailed on the street or found at designated taxi stands. Buses, known as "chivas," are colorful open-air vehicles that operate on set routes and are a more economical option. They are often used by locals and provide a unique way to experience the island's landscapes and culture.

e. Bicycles and Electric Scooters

Exploring the Galápagos on two wheels is a popular and eco-friendly option. Many towns and accommodations offer bicycle rentals, allowing you to explore the islands at your own pace. Bicycles are particularly suitable for Santa Cruz and San Cristóbal islands, where the terrain is relatively flat and the distances between attractions are manageable. Additionally, some places offer electric scooter rentals, which can be a fun and efficient way to get around.

f. Guided Tours

Joining guided tours is an excellent way to maximize your time and experience the highlights of the Galápagos Islands. Many tour operators provide transportation as part of their packages, taking care of inter-island transfers and transportation to various attractions. These tours often include knowledgeable guides who provide insights into the local wildlife and ecosystems. It's advisable to research and book tours in advance to secure your spot, especially during peak travel seasons.

g. Walking

One of the simplest and most rewarding ways to explore the Galápagos Islands is on foot. Walking allows you to immerse yourself in the natural beauty of the islands and encounter wildlife up close. Many of the main attractions, such as the Charles Darwin Research Station and Tortuga

Bay on Santa Cruz Island, are easily accessible by foot. However, it's important to follow designated trails and adhere to the guidelines set by the Galápagos National Park to minimize your impact on the delicate ecosystems.

Tips for Getting Around

- Plan your transportation in advance, especially for inter-island flights and tours.
- Check the schedules and make reservations for public boats and inter-island flights to secure your preferred dates and times.
- Be prepared for potential schedule changes or delays, as weather conditions can affect transportation in the Galápagos.
- Pack a day bag with essentials like water, snacks, sunscreen, and insect repellent for your excursions.
- Respect the rules and regulations of the Galápagos National Park, such as staying on designated trails and keeping a safe distance from wildlife.

This page was left blank intentionally

The Best Time to Visit for Honeymoon

Planning a honeymoon is an exciting and romantic endeavor, and choosing the right time to visit your dream destination is crucial. If you're considering the Galápagos Islands as your honeymoon destination, it's important to understand the best time to visit to ensure you have a memorable and enjoyable experience. In this chapter, I will provide you with detailed information about the best time to visit the Galápagos for a honeymoon, taking into account weather conditions, wildlife sightings, and other factors that can enhance your romantic getaway.

Understanding the Seasons in the Galápagos

The Galápagos Islands have two main seasons: the dry season (June to December) and the wet season (January to May). Each season offers unique experiences and attractions, so it's essential to consider your preferences and priorities when choosing the best time for your honeymoon.

Dry Season (June to December)

The dry season in the Galápagos is characterized by cooler temperatures and lower humidity. It is also the peak tourist season, mainly because of the presence of the Galápagos penguins, sea lions, and marine iguanas. The weather during this season is typically dry and sunny, with occasional showers. The water temperatures are cooler, making it ideal for snorkeling and diving enthusiasts.

The dry season is an excellent time for honeymooners who wish to explore the islands' underwater wonders and witness unique wildlife in their natural habitats. It provides ample opportunities for activities such as hiking, snorkeling, and kayaking. Additionally, the sea conditions are generally calmer, making boat excursions more pleasant.

Wet Season (January to May)

The wet season in the Galápagos is characterized by warmer temperatures and higher humidity. This season is known for its lush green landscapes and vibrant flora. Although it is considered the off-peak tourist season, it offers its own set of attractions and advantages for honeymooners.

During the wet season, the Galápagos Islands experience occasional rain showers and cloudy skies. However, these conditions create breathtaking landscapes and provide a refreshing atmosphere. The warmer water temperatures make swimming and snorkeling more enjoyable, and the presence of sea turtles, colorful fish, and vibrant marine life adds to the allure.

Wildlife enthusiasts will appreciate the wet season as it coincides with the breeding season for many species, including sea turtles, sea lions, and marine iguanas. This season offers unique opportunities to witness courtship rituals and nesting activities, adding a touch of romance and natural wonder to your honeymoon experience.

Choosing the Best Time for Your Honeymoon

When deciding on the best time to visit the Galápagos Islands for your honeymoon, consider the following factors:

a. **Your Preferences**: Reflect on your preferred activities and experiences. Are you more interested in wildlife encounters, snorkeling, or exploring the islands' landscapes? Understanding your preferences will help you align your honeymoon dates with the best season for those activities.

b. **Weather Conditions**: Evaluate your tolerance for different weather conditions. If you prefer drier and cooler weather, the dry season is ideal. However, if you enjoy lush greenery and don't mind occasional rain showers, the wet season can offer a unique and enchanting experience.

c. **Wildlife Sightings**: Consider the specific wildlife you wish to see during your honeymoon. If you have a particular interest in penguins, sea lions, or marine iguanas, the dry season is when they are most abundant and active.

d. **Budget and Crowds:** Keep in mind that the dry season is the peak tourist season, which means higher prices and more crowds. If you prefer a quieter and potentially more affordable honeymoon, the wet season might be a better option.

This page was left blank intentionally

The Best Time to Visit for Backpackers

The Galápagos Islands, with their unique wildlife and stunning landscapes, are a dream destination for backpackers seeking adventure and exploration. When planning your backpacking trip to the Galápagos, it's essential to consider the best time to visit to make the most of your experience. In this chapter, I will provide you with detailed information about the best time to visit the Galápagos for backpackers, taking into account factors such as weather, wildlife, and budget considerations.

Understanding the Seasons in the Galápagos

The Galápagos Islands have two main seasons: the dry season (June to December) and the wet season (January to May). Each season offers unique experiences and considerations for backpackers, and understanding them will help you plan your trip effectively.

Dry Season (June to December)

The dry season in the Galápagos is a popular time for backpackers due to the cooler temperatures and lower humidity. During this season, the weather is generally dry and sunny, with occasional showers. The water temperatures are cooler as well, making it an ideal time for snorkeling and diving.

One of the main advantages of visiting during the dry season is the abundance of wildlife sightings. You can expect to see iconic species such as Galápagos penguins, sea lions, and marine iguanas. The calm sea conditions during this season also make boat excursions more enjoyable.

Additionally, the dry season coincides with the peak tourist season, which means there will be more opportunities to connect with fellow travelers and engage in social activities. However, it's important to note that the dry season also brings higher prices for accommodations and activities.

Wet Season (January to May)

The wet season in the Galápagos is characterized by warmer temperatures and higher humidity. Although it's considered the off-peak tourist season, the wet season offers its own unique advantages for backpackers.

During this season, the Galápagos Islands are transformed into lush green landscapes. The occasional rain showers contribute to the vibrant flora, creating a picturesque setting for hiking and exploring the islands. The warmer water temperatures also make swimming and snorkeling more enjoyable.

Wildlife enthusiasts will appreciate the wet season as it coincides with the breeding season for many species, including sea turtles, sea lions, and marine iguanas. This provides backpackers with unique opportunities to witness these natural wonders and engage in wildlife conservation activities.

Choosing the Best Time for Your Backpacking Trip

When determining the best time to visit the Galápagos Islands for your backpacking adventure, consider the following factors:

- **Weather Conditions:** Evaluate your tolerance for different weather conditions. If you prefer drier and cooler weather, the dry season is the best choice. However, if you don't mind occasional rain showers and enjoy the lush greenery of the wet season, it can provide a more visually captivating experience.

- **Wildlife Sightings**: Consider the specific wildlife you wish to encounter during your backpacking trip. If you have a particular interest in certain species or want to witness breeding activities, the wet season offers greater opportunities for wildlife sightings.

- **Budget Considerations**: Keep in mind that the dry season is the peak tourist season, which means higher prices for accommodations and activities. If you're on a tighter budget, visiting during the wet season may offer more affordable options.

- **Crowds and Social Opportunities**: The dry season attracts more tourists, which can result in larger crowds. If you're looking to connect with fellow backpackers and engage in social activities, the dry season may provide more opportunities for socializing and meeting like-minded travelers.

This page was left blank intentionally

The Best Time to Visit for Different Travelers

The Galápagos Islands, known for their stunning biodiversity and unique wildlife, offer a remarkable travel experience for a wide range of travelers. Whether you are a nature enthusiast, a beach lover, a wildlife photographer, or a family seeking adventure, choosing the best time to visit the Galápagos is essential to ensure you have a memorable and tailored experience. In this chapter, I will explore the best time to visit the Galápagos Islands for different types of travelers, taking into account factors such as weather, wildlife, activities, and crowd levels.

Nature Enthusiasts

For nature enthusiasts, the best time to visit the Galápagos Islands is during the dry season, which lasts from June to December. This season offers favorable weather conditions with lower humidity and cooler temperatures, making it comfortable for outdoor activities. The dry season is also the peak time for wildlife sightings, including sea turtles, sea lions, and various bird species. The calm sea conditions during this season are perfect for snorkeling, diving, and exploring the islands' marine life.

Beach Lovers

If you are a beach lover and want to soak up the sun and relax on pristine beaches, the best time to visit the Galápagos Islands is during the warm and sunny months of the dry season. From June to December, you can enjoy the beautiful white sand beaches, crystal-clear waters, and a tranquil atmosphere. The water temperatures are cooler during this season, making it refreshing for swimming and snorkeling.

Wildlife Photographers

For wildlife photographers, the best time to visit the Galápagos Islands depends on the specific species you want to capture in your photographs. The dry season, particularly from July to September, is excellent for capturing images of iconic wildlife such as Galápagos penguins, blue-footed boobies, and giant tortoises. If you are interested in capturing breeding and nesting activities, the wet season from January to May provides unique opportunities.

Families

Families traveling with children often prefer visiting the Galápagos Islands during school vacations or holiday periods. The best time for family travel is during the dry season, particularly from June to August and in December. These months coincide with summer vacations in many countries, allowing families to spend quality time together and explore the islands' natural wonders. The dry season offers a wide range of activities suitable for children, such as snorkeling, hiking, and visiting nature reserves.

Adventure Seekers

If you are an adventure seeker looking for thrilling experiences in the Galápagos Islands, the best time to visit depends on the specific activities you want to pursue. The dry season offers ideal conditions for activities like snorkeling, diving, kayaking, and hiking. The calmer sea conditions during this season make water-based activities more enjoyable. However, adventure activities can be pursued throughout the year, and the wet season also offers its own set of adventures, such as exploring the lush landscapes and witnessing unique wildlife behaviors.

Budget Travelers

For budget-conscious travelers, the best time to visit the Galápagos Islands is during the wet season, particularly from January to May. This period is considered the off-peak tourist season, which means lower prices for accommodations and activities. Although there may be occasional rain showers during the wet season, the lush greenery and unique wildlife sightings make it a worthwhile time to visit, especially for those seeking a more affordable travel experience.

Diving Enthusiasts

If diving is your primary interest, the best time to visit the Galápagos Islands is during the dry season, particularly from June to November. The water visibility is typically at its best during this time, offering excellent opportunities for underwater exploration. The chance to encounter hammerhead sharks, whale sharks, and other large marine species is higher during the dry season, making it a diver's paradise.

Seasons in Galápagos

Understanding the different seasons in the Galápagos is essential for planning your trip, as each season presents distinct weather patterns, wildlife sightings, and opportunities for exploration. In this chapter, I will delve into the four seasons of Galápagos—spring, summer, autumn, and winter—to provide you with detailed information about what to expect during each season.

Galápagos in the Spring

Spring in the Galápagos Islands falls between September and November. During this season, the islands experience a transition from the cool and dry conditions of the dry season to warmer temperatures and occasional rain showers. Here are some key features of Galápagos in the spring:

Weather: Spring brings a gradual increase in temperature, with average highs ranging from 25 to 28°C (77 to 82°F). However, it's still relatively dry compared to the wet season. Expect occasional rain showers, but they are usually short-lived.

Wildlife: Spring is a prime time for marine life in the Galápagos. Sea turtles begin nesting on the beaches, and various bird species, including blue-footed boobies and waved albatrosses, engage in elaborate courtship displays. You can also witness the breeding season of sea lions and fur seals.

Underwater Activities: The waters are warm and inviting during the spring season, making it an excellent time for snorkeling and diving. The increased water temperatures attract a diverse array of marine species, including manta rays, dolphins, and schools of tropical fish.

Vegetation: The arrival of spring brings the islands to life with vibrant vegetation. The landscape becomes greener, and endemic plants such as the Galápagos cotton and scalesia trees flourish.

Galápagos in the Summer

The summer season in the Galápagos Islands spans from December to February. It is characterized by warmer temperatures, occasional rain showers, and a peak in tourist activity. Here's what you can expect during the summer season:

Weather: Summer brings the warmest temperatures of the year, with average highs ranging from 28 to 30°C (82 to 86°F). Humidity levels also increase, and brief rain showers are more common.

Wildlife: The summer season is known for its unique wildlife sightings. Green sea turtles hatch and make their way to the ocean, providing a remarkable spectacle. Galápagos penguins, the only penguin species found north of the equator, can be observed in their natural habitat. Additionally, seabirds such as frigatebirds and swallow-tailed gulls engage in their breeding activities.

Snorkeling and Diving: The waters during the summer are rich in nutrients, attracting an abundance of marine life. Snorkeling and diving activities offer opportunities to encounter playful sea lions, marine iguanas, and schools of colorful fish. The visibility underwater is generally good, allowing for breathtaking experiences.

Crowds: The summer season coincides with the holiday period in many countries, leading to a higher influx of tourists. Popular sites may be more crowded, and it's advisable to book accommodations and activities in advance.

Galápagos in the Autumn

Autumn in the Galápagos Islands extends from March to May. It is a transition period characterized by mild temperatures, occasional rain showers, and unique wildlife experiences. Here's what you can look forward to during autumn:

Weather: Autumn brings moderate temperatures, with average highs ranging from 26 to 28°C (79 to 82°F). The humidity levels begin to decrease, and rain showers become less frequent.

Wildlife: Autumn marks the end of the wet season and the beginning of the dry season. Land bird species, such as Darwin's finches, engage in nesting activities, while sea birds, including Nazca boobies and red-footed boobies, start their courtship rituals. Giant tortoises can be spotted migrating to the lower elevations of the islands.

Land Exploration: The comfortable temperatures and lush green landscapes of autumn make it an ideal time for hiking and exploring the unique flora and fauna on the islands. Witness the blooming of endemic plants and enjoy picturesque landscapes.

Water Activities: While the water temperature may still be warm, the visibility may vary due to plankton blooms.

However, this can attract larger marine species, such as whale sharks, offering thrilling encounters for snorkelers and divers.

Galápagos in the Winter

Winter in the Galápagos Islands falls between June and August. It is characterized by cooler temperatures, dry conditions, and a peak in wildlife activity. Here's what you can expect during the winter season:

Weather: Winter brings cooler temperatures, with average highs ranging from 23 to 25°C (73 to 77°F). The weather is generally dry, and the sea conditions are calm.

Wildlife: Winter is considered the peak season for wildlife sightings in the Galápagos Islands. It offers excellent opportunities to witness the iconic species that the archipelago is renowned for, including marine iguanas, Galápagos penguins, and waved albatrosses. Giant tortoises can be seen mating, and sea lion pups are abundant on the beaches.

Snorkeling and Diving: The calm sea conditions during winter provide exceptional visibility for snorkeling and diving. Encounter playful sea lions, sea turtles, and an array of colorful fish in the pristine waters of the Galápagos.

Crowds: Winter is the busiest tourist season in the Galápagos Islands. Popular sites may be crowded, and it's advisable to book accommodations and activities well in advance to secure your preferred options.

This page was left blank intentionally

A Month-to-Month Guide to Visiting Galápagos

From wildlife encounters to weather conditions, each month in Galápagos has its own charm. In this chapter, I will explore the Galápagos Islands month by month, providing you with insights and recommendations for your visit.

Galápagos in January

January marks the beginning of the wet season in the Galápagos Islands. While the occasional rain showers may occur, they are typically short-lived. Here's what you can expect during January:

Weather: January experiences warm temperatures, with average highs ranging from 28 to 30°C (82 to 86°F). The sea temperatures are pleasant for swimming and water activities.

Wildlife: January is a fantastic time for wildlife enthusiasts. Witness the courtship rituals of marine iguanas, as they change color to attract mates. Sea lion pups can be spotted on the beaches, and various bird species, including blue-footed boobies and frigatebirds, engage in elaborate displays.

Snorkeling and Diving: The underwater world comes alive in January. Snorkelers and divers have the opportunity to encounter playful sea lions, sea turtles, and an array of colorful fish.

Vegetation: The vegetation is lush and vibrant, with an abundance of blooming flowers and foliage.

Galápagos in February

February continues the wet season in the Galápagos Islands, with occasional rain showers and warm temperatures. Here's what you can look forward to in February:

Wildlife: February is a peak time for wildlife activity. Witness the courtship dances of blue-footed boobies and the impressive mating displays of waved albatrosses on Española Island. Sea lions continue to give birth, and you may spot newborn pups on the shores.

Marine Life: The waters around the Galápagos Islands are teeming with life in February. Snorkelers and divers can encounter playful sea lions, turtles, and various species of rays.

Bird Nesting: February is the nesting season for several bird species, including Nazca boobies and red-footed boobies. Visitors can observe the intricate mating rituals and nesting behaviors of these fascinating birds.

Weather: The weather in February remains warm, with average highs ranging from 28 to 30°C (82 to 86°F). Be prepared for occasional rain showers, but they are usually short-lived.

Galápagos in March

March marks the transition period between the wet and dry seasons in the Galápagos Islands. The weather becomes drier, and the sea conditions are generally calm. Here's what you can expect during March:

Wildlife: March is an exciting time for wildlife sightings. Witness the hatching of giant tortoise eggs, and observe their journey as they make their way to the highlands. Spot land iguanas as they nest and the emergence of new hatchlings.

Migratory Birds: March is when migratory birds, such as swallow-tailed gulls and red-billed tropicbirds, arrive in the Galápagos Islands. The skies are filled with these beautiful birds, adding to the vibrant birdlife of the archipelago.

Snorkeling and Diving: The waters are clear and calm in March, making it an ideal time for underwater activities.

Encounter playful sea lions, sea turtles, and an array of colorful fish.

Weather: The weather in March is pleasant, with average highs ranging from 27 to 29°C (81 to 84°F). The humidity levels are lower compared to the previous months.

Galápagos in April

April marks the beginning of the dry season in the Galápagos Islands. The weather becomes cooler, and the skies are often clear. Here's what you can look forward to in April:

Wildlife: April offers fantastic wildlife encounters. Witness the courtship rituals of blue-footed boobies as they perform their unique dance to attract mates. Spot sea lion pups playing in the turquoise waters and sea turtles nesting on the beaches.

Snorkeling and Diving: April offers excellent snorkeling and diving conditions. The visibility underwater is usually excellent, allowing for incredible encounters with marine life such as hammerhead sharks, eagle rays, and schools of tropical fish.

Land Exploration: The dry season is a great time for land exploration and hiking. The vegetation is lush, and the landscapes are picturesque. Take a hike to the volcanic craters or explore the highlands to observe giant tortoises in their natural habitat.

Weather: April experiences cooler temperatures, with average highs ranging from 26 to 28°C (79 to 82°F). The trade winds bring a refreshing breeze, making it comfortable for outdoor activities.

Galápagos in May

May continues the dry season in the Galápagos Islands, with cooler temperatures and occasional showers. Here's what you can expect during May:

Wildlife: May offers incredible opportunities for wildlife enthusiasts. Witness the fascinating courtship dances of Nazca boobies, as they compete for mates. Observe land iguanas as they bask in the sun and marine iguanas nesting on the rocky shores.

Birdwatching: May is a prime time for birdwatching in the Galápagos Islands. Spot the magnificent waved albatross on Española Island, as they perform their elaborate courtship rituals. This is the only place in the world where these impressive birds breed.

Snorkeling and Diving: The water temperature in May remains pleasant, making it a great time for snorkeling and diving. Encounter playful sea lions, sea turtles, and a variety of fish species in the crystal-clear waters.

Weather: May experiences cooler temperatures, with average highs ranging from 25 to 27°C (77 to 81°F). Be prepared for occasional showers, but they are usually brief.

Galápagos in June

June marks the beginning of the cool and dry season in the Galápagos Islands. The weather becomes cooler, and the Humboldt Current brings nutrient-rich waters to the archipelago. Here's what you can look forward to in June:

Wildlife: June offers incredible wildlife encounters. Witness the courtship displays of magnificent frigatebirds, as the males inflate their vibrant red throat pouches to attract mates. Spot marine iguanas in their colorful breeding colors and sea lions nursing their newborn pups.

Whale Watching: June is a prime time for whale watching in the Galápagos Islands. Humpback whales migrate to the warm waters of the archipelago to breed and give birth. Visitors have the opportunity to witness these majestic creatures breaching and tail-slapping.

Land Exploration: The cooler temperatures in June make it an ideal time for land exploration and hiking. Explore the volcanic landscapes, visit lava tunnels, and encounter unique vegetation, including the endemic scalesia trees.

Weather: June experiences cooler temperatures, with average highs ranging from 24 to 26°C (75 to 79°F). The sea conditions are generally calm, offering smooth sailing and excellent visibility for water activities.

Galápagos in July

July continues the cool and dry season in the Galápagos Islands. The Humboldt Current brings cooler waters and an abundance of marine life to the archipelago. Here's what you can expect during July:

Wildlife: July offers exceptional wildlife sightings. Witness the unique mating rituals of Galápagos penguins, the only penguin species found north of the equator. Spot playful sea lion pups learning to swim and hunt.

Marine Life: The cooler waters in July attract a diverse range of marine species. Snorkelers and divers can encounter sea turtles, colorful reef fish, and even sharks. The nutrient-rich currents also bring in large schools of fish, creating a vibrant underwater ecosystem.

Birdwatching: July is a fantastic time for birdwatching, with numerous species in their nesting and breeding season. Spot the iconic blue-footed boobies, Galápagos hawks, and the red-billed tropicbirds with their elegant long tail feathers.

Weather: July experiences cooler temperatures, with average highs ranging from 23 to 25°C (73 to 77°F). The nights can be cooler, so it's advisable to pack some warmer layers.

Galápagos in August

August marks the peak of the cool and dry season in the Galápagos Islands. The waters are at their coolest, and wildlife activity is abundant. Here's what you can look forward to in August:

Wildlife: August offers incredible wildlife encounters. Witness the impressive courtship rituals of waved albatrosses on Española Island, as they engage in bill-fencing and beak-clacking displays. Spot sea lions basking in the sun, and observe blue-footed boobies feeding their chicks.

Marine Life: August is an excellent time for snorkeling and diving. The colder waters attract various marine species, including reef sharks, sea turtles, and large schools of fish. It's also a prime time to encounter playful sea lions underwater.

Land Exploration: The dry landscapes of the Galápagos Islands provide excellent opportunities for land exploration. Hike to viewpoints for panoramic views of the archipelago, and explore lava formations and unique vegetation.

Weather: August experiences cooler temperatures, with average highs ranging from 23 to 25°C (73 to 77°F). The sea conditions are generally calm, providing smooth sailing and clear visibility for water activities.

Galápagos in September

September marks the end of the cool and dry season in the Galápagos Islands. The weather starts to transition, with warmer temperatures and occasional showers. Here's what you can expect during September:

Wildlife: September offers a mix of wildlife experiences. Witness the courtship rituals of blue-footed boobies, as they perform their elaborate dance to attract mates. Observe land iguanas as they feed on cacti, and spot Galápagos hawks soaring above.

Sea Lion Mating Season: September is the start of the sea lion mating season. Male sea lions compete for dominance and breeding rights, displaying their strength and agility. Witness these impressive displays on the beaches.

Snorkeling and Diving: September offers excellent snorkeling and diving conditions. Encounter sea turtles, colorful reef fish, and potentially large schools of hammerhead sharks. The water visibility is usually good, providing memorable underwater experiences.

Weather: September experiences warmer temperatures, with average highs ranging from 24 to 26°C (75 to 79°F). Be prepared for occasional rain showers, but they are usually short-lived.

Galápagos in October

October marks the transition from the dry to the wet season in the Galápagos Islands. The weather becomes warmer, and the occasional rain showers increase. Here's what you can look forward to in October:

Wildlife: October offers a mix of wildlife experiences. Witness the nesting activities of Nazca boobies, as they lay their eggs and care for their young. Spot colorful Sally

Lightfoot crabs on the shores, and observe the interactions between marine iguanas.

Tortoise Mating Season: October marks the beginning of the giant tortoise mating season. Spot male tortoises engaging in territorial disputes and courtship behaviors. Witness these magnificent creatures in their natural habitat.

Birdwatching: October is a great time for birdwatching, with various species in their breeding season. Spot the elegant great frigatebirds with their inflated red throat pouches, and observe Galápagos doves and finches in their natural habitat.

Weather: October experiences warmer temperatures, with average highs ranging from 25 to 27°C (77 to 81°F). The humidity levels increase, and occasional rain showers can be expected.

Galápagos in November

November marks the beginning of the wet season in the Galápagos Islands, with occasional rain showers and warmer temperatures. Here's what you can expect during November:

Wildlife: November offers unique wildlife encounters. Observe the courtship rituals of blue-footed boobies, as they display their vibrant feet to attract mates. Witness the nesting activities of green sea turtles, and spot sea lion pups learning to swim.

Plant Life: November brings a burst of greenery to the Galápagos Islands. The vegetation is lush, and various plants and trees bloom with colorful flowers.

Snorkeling and Diving: November offers good snorkeling and diving conditions. Encounter sea turtles, sea lions, and a variety of fish species in the clear waters. The nutrient-rich currents also attract larger marine species, such as sharks and rays.

Weather: November experiences warmer temperatures, with average highs ranging from 26 to 28°C (79 to 82°F). Be prepared for occasional rain showers, but they are usually short-lived.

Galápagos in December

December marks the peak of the wet season in the Galápagos Islands. The vegetation is lush, and the wildlife activity is abundant. Here's what you can look forward to in December:

Wildlife: December offers incredible wildlife encounters. Witness the mating rituals of waved albatrosses on Española Island, as they engage in their elaborate displays. Spot sea lion pups playing in the shallow waters, and observe colorful marine iguanas feeding on algae.

Birdwatching: December is a prime time for birdwatching, with various species in their breeding season. Spot

Galápagos penguins, flightless cormorants, and blue-footed boobies, among others.

Snorkeling and Diving: December offers excellent snorkeling and diving conditions. Encounter sea turtles, playful sea lions, and an array of vibrant fish species. The underwater visibility is usually good, providing memorable underwater experiences.

Weather: December experiences warm temperatures, with average highs ranging from 27 to 29°C (81 to 84°F). The humidity levels are higher, and occasional rain showers can be expected.

This page was left blank intentionally

Essentials Packs for Galápagos

When planning a trip to the Galápagos Islands, it's important to pack wisely to ensure you have all the essentials for a comfortable and enjoyable experience. The remote and unique nature of the islands requires some specific items that will enhance your adventure. Here are the essential packs you should consider for your Galápagos journey:

Clothing:

- **Lightweight and breathable clothing**: Pack lightweight and breathable clothing suitable for the warm and humid climate of the islands. Opt for moisture-wicking fabrics that dry quickly.
- **Swimsuits**: Don't forget to pack your swimsuits for snorkeling, swimming, and enjoying the beautiful beaches.
- **Comfortable walking shoes**: Choose comfortable walking shoes or hiking sandals for exploring the islands' trails and volcanic terrain.

- **Hat and sunglasses**: Protect yourself from the sun by packing a wide-brimmed hat and sunglasses with UV protection.
- **Lightweight rain jacket**: While the Galápagos Islands are generally dry, it's always a good idea to pack a lightweight rain jacket in case of unexpected showers.

Sun Protection:

- **Sunscreen**: The Galápagos Islands are located near the equator, so it's crucial to pack a high SPF sunscreen to protect your skin from the intense sun rays.
- **After-sun lotion**: In case of sunburn, pack a soothing after-sun lotion to provide relief and aid in skin recovery.
- **Lip balm with SPF:** Don't forget to protect your lips from the sun's rays with a lip balm containing SPF.
- **Snorkel mask and fins:** While some tours and cruises provide snorkeling gear, having your own

well-fitted mask and fins ensures comfort and hygiene.
- **Rash guard or wetsuit:** Depending on your preference and the time of year you visit, consider packing a rash guard or shorty wetsuit for extended snorkeling sessions or to protect against jellyfish stings.

Essential Accessories:

- **Waterproof bag:** Protect your valuables and electronic devices by packing a waterproof bag or dry bag.
- **Binoculars:** Bring a pair of binoculars to enhance your wildlife-watching experience, allowing you to observe birds, sea lions, and other marine creatures from a distance.
- **Camera or GoPro**: Capture the unforgettable moments and unique wildlife encounters in the Galápagos Islands by packing a camera or GoPro with extra batteries and memory cards.

Medications and First Aid:

Prescription medications: If you take any prescription medications, ensure you have an ample supply for the duration of your trip.

- **Motion sickness medication**: If you are prone to motion sickness, consider packing motion sickness medication for boat trips.
- **First aid kit:** Prepare a small first aid kit with essential items such as band-aids, antiseptic ointment, pain relievers, and any necessary personal medications.

Miscellaneous Items:

- **Reusable water bottle**: Stay hydrated by bringing a reusable water bottle. The tap water in the Galápagos Islands is safe to drink.
- **Insect repellent**: Although mosquitoes are not prevalent in the Galápagos, it's advisable to pack a small bottle of insect repellent for any encounters with insects on the islands.
- **Cash and credit cards:** While credit cards are accepted in some places, it's recommended to carry

some cash for smaller establishments and to pay for park fees.

Remember to pack light and efficiently, considering the luggage restrictions imposed by airlines and cruise operators in the Galápagos Islands. It's also essential to respect the fragile ecosystem of the islands by avoiding single-use plastics and disposing of waste properly.

By packing these essential items, you'll be well-prepared to make the most of your Galápagos adventure, ensuring comfort, protection, and memorable experiences in this remarkable destination.

This page was left blank intentionally

The Most Necessary Items

When planning a trip to the Galápagos Islands, it's important to prioritize the most necessary items to ensure a smooth and enjoyable experience. While packing, consider the unique environment and activities the islands offer. Here are the most necessary items you should bring:

Travel Documents:

- **Passport**: Ensure your passport is valid for at least six months beyond your intended stay in the Galápagos Islands.
- **Travel insurance**: Protect yourself against unexpected situations by having travel insurance that covers medical emergencies, trip cancellations, and lost luggage.
- **Itinerary and reservation details**: Keep a printed copy or electronic version of your travel itinerary, accommodation reservations, and any tour or activity bookings.

Money and Banking:

- **Local currency**: Bring some cash in US dollars, as it is widely accepted in the Galápagos Islands. Ensure you have small denominations for smaller establishments and tipping.
- **Credit/debit cards**: Carry at least one major credit card or debit card that can be used internationally. Notify your bank about your travel plans to avoid any issues with card usage.

Medications and Health Essentials:

- **Prescription medications**: If you require prescription medications, ensure you have an adequate supply for the duration of your trip, along with any necessary documentation.
- **Personal health items**: Pack any necessary personal health items such as prescription glasses, contact lenses, contact lens solution, and any essential over-the-counter medications.
- **Basic first aid kit**: Include items such as band-aids, antiseptic ointment, pain relievers, motion sickness

pills, and any specific medications or medical supplies you may need.

Essential Electronics:

- **Mobile phone and charger**: Bring your mobile phone and charger to stay connected and for emergencies. Check with your service provider about international roaming options or consider purchasing a local SIM card.
- **Camera or GoPro:** Capture the incredible sights and wildlife encounters in the Galápagos Islands. Make sure to bring spare batteries, memory cards, and charging accessories.

Personal Care Items:

- **Toiletries**: Pack travel-sized toiletries such as toothbrush, toothpaste, shampoo, conditioner, soap, and any other personal care items you require.
- **Insect repellent:** While mosquitoes are not prevalent in the Galápagos Islands, it's still advisable to bring insect repellent to protect against any biting insects.

Clothing and Accessories:

- **Comfortable and breathable clothing**: Pack lightweight and quick-drying clothing suitable for the warm and humid climate of the islands. Include a mix of short-sleeved and long-sleeved shirts, shorts, pants, swimsuits, and comfortable walking shoes.
- **Hat and sunglasses**: Protect yourself from the strong sun with a wide-brimmed hat and sunglasses with UV protection.
- **Rain jacket or poncho**: Although rain showers are infrequent, it's wise to bring a lightweight rain jacket or poncho for unexpected weather changes.

Snorkeling Gear:

- **Snorkel mask and fins**: While some tours and cruises provide snorkeling gear, consider bringing your own for a better fit and hygiene purposes.

- **Rash guard or wetsuit**: Depending on the time of year and personal preference, a rash guard or shorty wetsuit can provide extra comfort and protection during snorkeling sessions.

Miscellaneous Items:

- **Reusable water bottle**: Stay hydrated by bringing a reusable water bottle. The tap water in the Galápagos Islands is safe to drink.
- **Waterproof bag or dry bag**: Protect your belongings, electronics, and important documents from water damage by using a waterproof bag or dry bag.
- **Binoculars:** Enhance your wildlife-watching experience by bringing a pair of binoculars to spot birds, marine creatures, and distant wildlife.
- **Travel adapter**: The Galápagos Islands use standard US electrical outlets, so if you are traveling from a different region, bring a travel adapter to charge your devices.

This page was left blank intentionally

Is Galápagos safe in the night?

The safety of Galápagos at night is an important consideration for travelers visiting this unique archipelago. While Galápagos is generally a safe destination, it's essential to be aware of certain factors to ensure a secure experience during nighttime activities. Here's a comprehensive overview of the safety in Galápagos at night:

Crime Rate:

Galápagos has a relatively low crime rate compared to many other tourist destinations. Violent crimes are rare, and most incidents are opportunistic thefts or petty crimes. However, it's important to exercise caution and follow general safety guidelines to minimize the risk of becoming a target.

Personal Safety:

When exploring Galápagos at night, it's advisable to stay in well-lit and populated areas. Stick to main roads and avoid wandering into isolated or unfamiliar neighborhoods. Traveling in groups can enhance personal safety, especially when venturing out after dark.

Transportation:

If you need to travel at night in Galápagos, it's recommended to use reputable and licensed taxi services or arrange transportation through your accommodation. Avoid accepting rides from unmarked vehicles or strangers. Ensure that the vehicle is in good condition and has seat belts for your safety.

Street Lighting:

While some towns and developed areas in Galápagos have adequate street lighting, it's important to note that the islands' infrastructure may vary. In more remote or rural areas, the level of street lighting may be limited. Be cautious when walking in poorly lit areas and use a flashlight if necessary.

Wildlife Encounters:

One unique aspect of Galápagos is its abundant wildlife, which includes various species of animals and birds. While these encounters can be thrilling, it's crucial to maintain a safe distance and avoid disturbing or approaching the wildlife, especially at night. Respect the guidelines provided by your guides or the National Park authorities to ensure both your safety and the preservation of the natural habitat.

Natural Hazards:

Galápagos is a volcanic archipelago, and certain areas may have uneven terrain or volcanic features. Exercise caution when exploring natural sites at night, such as lava fields or coastal areas, to avoid accidents or falls. It's advisable to hire a licensed guide who is familiar with the terrain and can provide necessary safety guidance.

Responsible Behavior:

Practicing responsible behavior is crucial for your safety and the preservation of the delicate ecosystem. Avoid littering, as it can attract unwanted wildlife and disrupt the natural balance. Follow all rules and regulations of the Galápagos National Park, including staying on designated paths and respecting the local flora and fauna.

Emergency Preparedness:

It's always important to be prepared for emergencies, regardless of the time of day. Familiarize yourself with the location of emergency services, including hospitals, clinics, and police stations. Keep emergency contact numbers handy and ensure you have appropriate travel insurance that covers medical emergencies.

Local Advice and Guidance:

Seek advice and guidance from local authorities, your accommodation providers, or licensed tour operators regarding safety precautions and specific risks associated with nighttime activities in the Galápagos Islands. They can provide valuable insights and recommendations to enhance your safety and overall experience.

While Galápagos is generally considered safe at night, it's crucial to exercise caution and use common sense. By staying aware of your surroundings, following local advice, and respecting the natural environment, you can have a safe and memorable experience exploring the beauty of Galápagos after dark.

Is it safe to Visit Galápagos?

With its stunning landscapes, diverse wildlife, and protected natural areas, Galápagos attracts visitors from around the world. However, it's important to be aware of certain factors to ensure a safe and enjoyable experience. In this chapter, I will explore the safety aspects of visiting Galápagos.

Low Crime Rate:

Galápagos has a relatively low crime rate compared to many other tourist destinations. Violent crimes are rare, and most incidents reported are non-violent in nature, such as opportunistic thefts or petty crimes. However, it's always wise to exercise caution and take necessary precautions to avoid becoming a target.

Tourist Police and Security Measures:

The Galápagos National Police and Tourist Police play an important role in maintaining safety and security on the islands. They patrol popular tourist areas, monitor activities, and assist visitors when needed. These authorities work closely with the Galápagos National Park and local communities to ensure the well-being of tourists.

Natural Hazards:

While Galápagos offers breathtaking natural beauty, it's essential to be aware of potential hazards. The islands are of volcanic origin, and certain areas may have uneven terrain or active volcanic features. It's important to follow safety guidelines, stay on designated paths, and heed the advice of licensed guides to prevent accidents.

Marine Safety:

Galápagos is renowned for its exceptional marine ecosystem, attracting snorkelers and divers from around the world. While exploring the underwater world, it's crucial to prioritize marine safety. Ensure you are in good health, have proper training and certification if required, and follow the instructions of experienced guides to enjoy safe and responsible marine activities.

Wildlife Interactions:

Galápagos is famous for its unique and abundant wildlife, including various bird species, marine mammals, and reptiles. While these wildlife encounters can be incredible, it's essential to maintain a safe distance and respect the animals' natural behavior. Interacting responsibly with wildlife ensures both your safety and the preservation of the fragile ecosystem.

Transportation Safety:

When traveling between islands or exploring different sites within Galápagos, it's important to prioritize transportation safety. Choose reputable tour operators or licensed boats and vessels that adhere to safety regulations. Ensure that life jackets and safety equipment are provided, and follow the instructions of the crew or guides during water-based activities.

Weather and Environmental Conditions:

Galápagos experiences various weather conditions throughout the year, including strong sun, occasional rain, and sometimes rough seas. It's essential to prepare accordingly, bring appropriate clothing and accessories, and stay informed about weather forecasts. Pay attention to any safety advisories issued by the authorities, especially during extreme weather events.

Health and Medical Facilities:

Galápagos has medical facilities and clinics to address common health issues and emergencies. However, for more serious medical conditions, evacuation to the mainland may be necessary. It's advisable to have travel insurance that covers medical expenses and repatriation, and to carry any necessary medications or prescriptions.

Environmental Responsibility:

As a visitor to Galápagos, it's crucial to embrace environmental responsibility. Respect the protected areas, follow the guidelines of the Galápagos National Park, and refrain from littering. Minimize your ecological footprint and avoid disturbing the natural habitats and wildlife. By being a responsible traveler, you contribute to the preservation of this unique ecosystem.

Local Guidance:

Seek advice and guidance from local authorities, your accommodation providers, or licensed tour operators. They can provide valuable information about safety precautions, specific risks associated with certain activities, and recommendations for a safe and enjoyable experience in Galápagos.

This page was left blank intentionally

Is Galápagos good for International Students?

Galápagos, with its unparalleled biodiversity and unique ecosystem, offers an incredible learning opportunity for international students. This archipelago, located in the Pacific Ocean, provides a one-of-a-kind environment for scientific research, conservation studies, and experiential learning. In this chapter, I will explore why Galápagos is an excellent destination for international students and the benefits they can gain from studying in this remarkable location.

Rich Biodiversity and Natural Laboratory:

Galápagos is renowned for its rich biodiversity, making it a natural laboratory for various fields of study. The archipelago is home to numerous endemic species, including the famous Galápagos tortoises, marine iguanas, and Darwin's finches. The diverse flora and fauna present ample opportunities for students to engage in field research, ecological studies, and conservation projects.

Unique Learning Opportunities:

Galápagos offers a unique learning environment that combines classroom instruction with hands-on fieldwork. International students can engage in a wide range of disciplines such as biology, ecology, marine sciences, geology, environmental studies, and sustainable tourism. The islands provide a living classroom where students can observe and study the natural world up close.

World-Class Research Institutions:

Galápagos is home to world-class research institutions and educational facilities that offer exceptional learning opportunities for international students. These institutions provide access to state-of-the-art laboratories, specialized equipment, and expert faculty members who are actively involved in research and conservation efforts. Students can collaborate on ongoing projects and contribute to scientific discoveries.

Environmental Conservation and Sustainability:

Galápagos has a strong focus on environmental conservation and sustainability. International students interested in these areas can actively participate in research projects and initiatives aimed at preserving the unique ecosystem. By studying in Galápagos, students can develop a deep understanding of the challenges faced by fragile ecosystems and contribute to their long-term preservation.

Cultural and Historical Significance:

Galápagos has significant historical and cultural importance, particularly in relation to Charles Darwin's theory of evolution. Studying in Galápagos offers students a chance to explore the natural wonders that inspired Darwin's groundbreaking ideas. They can visit historical sites, learn about the islands' human settlement, and gain insights into the cultural heritage of the local communities.

Experiential Learning and Field Trips:

Studying in Galápagos allows students to engage in experiential learning and field trips that provide hands-on experiences. They can participate in activities such as snorkeling, scuba diving, hiking, and wildlife observation, enabling them to directly interact with the unique flora and fauna of the islands. These experiences deepen their understanding of ecological processes and foster a sense of appreciation for nature.

Networking and Collaborations:

Galápagos attracts scientists, researchers, and conservationists from around the world, providing international students with valuable networking opportunities. Students can connect with experts in their respective fields, collaborate on research projects, and build professional relationships that may benefit their future careers. These connections can open doors to further academic pursuits or job opportunities in the field of conservation and environmental science.

Cultural Exchange and Global Perspective:

Studying in Galápagos offers international students the chance to immerse themselves in a diverse and multicultural environment. They can interact with students and researchers from different countries, fostering cultural exchange and gaining a global perspective on environmental issues. This exposure to diverse viewpoints enhances their intercultural competence and broadens their worldview.

Personal Growth and Resilience:

Living and studying in a remote and unique environment like Galápagos challenges students to adapt, be resourceful, and develop resilience. The island lifestyle encourages self-reliance, problem-solving skills, and a sense of adventure. Students become more independent, self-aware, and capable of overcoming challenges, which are valuable qualities for personal growth and future endeavors.

Career Advancement:

A study experience in Galápagos can significantly enhance the career prospects of international students. The knowledge, skills, and hands-on experience gained through studying in this unique environment are highly valued by employers, particularly in the fields of conservation, environmental science, research, and education. Graduates with Galápagos experience may have a competitive edge in their future careers.

This page was left blank intentionally

Tips and Tricks for Staying Safe in Galápagos

When visiting the enchanting Galápagos Islands, it's important to prioritize your safety to ensure a smooth and enjoyable experience. While Galápagos is generally a safe destination, it's always wise to be prepared and take necessary precautions. In this guide, we will provide you with a comprehensive list of tips and tricks to help you stay safe during your visit to Galápagos.

Research and Plan Ahead:

Before traveling to Galápagos, conduct thorough research about the islands, including the specific areas you plan to visit. Familiarize yourself with the local customs, regulations, and any potential risks or safety concerns. Plan your itinerary in advance, considering factors such as weather conditions, transportation options, and activities available.

Choose Reputable Tour Operators and Guides:

When engaging in tours and activities, select reputable tour operators and licensed guides. Look for companies with good reviews and a strong emphasis on safety. Ensure that they follow sustainable practices and adhere to the guidelines set by the Galápagos National Park. Licensed guides can provide valuable insights, ensure your safety during excursions, and enhance your overall experience.

Follow Park Rules and Guidelines:

The Galápagos National Park has specific rules and guidelines in place to protect the islands' fragile ecosystem. Respect these regulations and follow the instructions provided by park authorities and guides. Avoid disturbing wildlife, do not feed animals, and stay on designated trails to minimize your impact on the environment.

Stay Hydrated and Protect Yourself from the Sun:

Galápagos has a warm and sunny climate, so it's essential to stay hydrated and protect yourself from the sun's rays. Drink plenty of water, especially when engaging in outdoor activities, and carry a reusable water bottle. Apply sunscreen with a high SPF, wear a hat, and use sunglasses to protect your skin and eyes from the sun.

Be Cautious of Wildlife Interactions:

While Galápagos is famous for its unique wildlife, it's important to maintain a safe distance and respect the animals' natural behavior. Approaching too closely or attempting to touch wildlife can be harmful to both you and the animals. Follow the guidance of your guides and observe wildlife from a safe and respectful distance.

Use Reputable Transportation Services:

When moving between islands or exploring different sites, use reputable transportation services. Choose licensed boats, ferries, or airlines that prioritize safety and adhere to regulations. Check the safety records and reviews of transportation providers to ensure a reliable and secure journey.

Be Prepared for Outdoor Activities:

Galápagos offers a range of outdoor activities such as hiking, snorkeling, and diving. Ensure you have the necessary equipment, including sturdy footwear, appropriate swimwear, snorkeling gear, and a waterproof bag to protect your belongings. Follow the instructions of guides and instructors, and be aware of your own limitations and comfort level when participating in these activities.

Secure Your Belongings:

While Galápagos is relatively safe, it's still important to take precautions to protect your belongings. Keep your valuables secure at all times, preferably in a locked bag or hotel safe. Avoid displaying expensive jewelry or electronics that may attract unwanted attention. Be cautious in crowded areas and always keep an eye on your belongings.

Stay Informed about Weather Conditions:

Galápagos experiences different weather patterns throughout the year, including occasional rain and strong sun. Stay informed about weather conditions by checking forecasts and listening to updates from local authorities. Prepare accordingly with appropriate clothing, gear, and accessories to ensure your comfort and safety.

Respect Local Customs and Culture:

Embrace the local customs and culture of Galápagos during your visit. Respect the traditions, customs, and ways of life of the local communities. Dress modestly when visiting towns or villages, and be mindful of local sensitivities. Learning a few basic phrases in Spanish can also help you communicate and connect with the locals.

Maintain Personal Health and Safety:

Prioritize your personal health and safety during your stay in Galápagos. Stay hydrated, eat well-balanced meals, and carry any necessary medications or prescriptions. Follow basic hygiene practices, including washing your hands regularly and using insect repellent to prevent bites. If you have any specific health concerns, consult with a healthcare professional before traveling.

Stay Connected and Share Itinerary:

Maintain regular communication with your travel companions and inform someone back home about your itinerary. Share details of your accommodation, transportation, and contact information with a trusted person. Consider carrying a local SIM card or utilizing Wi-Fi hotspots to stay connected and have access to emergency services if needed.

Trust Your Instincts:

Finally, trust your instincts and be mindful of your surroundings. If a situation feels unsafe or uncomfortable, remove yourself from it. Pay attention to your intuition and exercise caution, particularly in unfamiliar areas or at night. Trusting your instincts is an essential part of ensuring your personal safety.

Is it safe for Solo Female to Travel to Galápagos

Traveling solo as a female can be an empowering and enriching experience, and Galápagos is generally considered a safe destination for solo female travelers. While it's always important to exercise caution and be aware of your surroundings, Galápagos offers a welcoming and secure environment for women exploring the islands. In this guide, we will discuss the safety considerations and tips for solo female travelers visiting Galápagos.

Safe and Welcoming Destination:

Galápagos has a reputation for being a safe and welcoming destination for travelers, including solo female travelers. The local communities are friendly, and tourism plays a vital role in the islands' economy. The islands' small size and close-knit communities contribute to a sense of security and a supportive atmosphere.

Low Crime Rates:

Galápagos has relatively low crime rates, including petty theft and violent crimes. However, it's still essential to take basic precautions, such as keeping an eye on your belongings and being mindful of your surroundings. Like any other destination, it's advisable to avoid displaying expensive jewelry or valuables that may attract unnecessary attention.

Respect Local Customs and Dress Modestly:

When traveling in Galápagos, it's important to respect the local customs and traditions. Dress modestly, particularly when visiting towns or villages, to show respect for the local culture. By adhering to local norms, you will blend in better and experience a more harmonious interaction with the local community.

Stay in Established Accommodations:

Choosing reputable and established accommodations can contribute to a safer experience for solo female travelers. Look for accommodations that have good reviews, prioritize security measures, and are located in well-populated areas. This ensures you have a safe and comfortable base during your stay.

Stay Connected and Inform Others:

Prioritize communication and stay connected with family, friends, or a trusted person during your solo trip to Galápagos. Share your travel itinerary, accommodation details, and contact information with someone back home. Regularly update them on your whereabouts and any changes to your plans. Consider carrying a local SIM card or using Wi-Fi hotspots to stay connected during your trip.

Research and Plan Your Itinerary:

Thorough research and planning are essential for a smooth and safe solo trip. Understand the geography, transportation options, and attractions in Galápagos. Plan your itinerary in advance, considering factors such as safety, accessibility, and timing. Be mindful of potential risks and safety concerns in specific areas and follow the advice of local authorities and guides.

Join Group Tours and Activities:

Participating in group tours and activities can enhance your safety as a solo female traveler. Group tours provide an opportunity to meet fellow travelers, share experiences, and have a sense of companionship. Choose reputable tour operators that prioritize safety and have knowledgeable guides who can provide insights and support throughout your excursions.

Trust Your Instincts:

Trusting your instincts is crucial when traveling solo. If a situation feels uncomfortable or unsafe, remove yourself from it. Listen to your intuition and prioritize your well-being. Avoid isolated areas at night and stick to well-lit and populated areas. It's essential to strike a balance between being adventurous and maintaining personal safety.

Connect with Other Travelers:

Solo female travelers can connect with other like-minded individuals, both locals and fellow travelers, during their time in Galápagos. Engage in conversations, join group activities, or connect through online travel communities or social media platforms. Sharing experiences and insights can provide a sense of camaraderie and additional safety.

Stay Informed about Local Laws and Regulations:

Familiarize yourself with the local laws, regulations, and cultural norms of Galápagos. Understanding the rules regarding protected areas, wildlife interactions, and responsible tourism practices will ensure you have a positive and respectful experience. Adhering to the guidelines and regulations contributes to the conservation efforts and helps maintain the integrity of the islands.

This page was left blank intentionally

Scams in Galápagos

When traveling to any destination, including Galápagos, it's essential to be aware of potential scams that could impact your experience. While Galápagos is generally a safe and reputable destination, it's important to be vigilant and informed about common scams that can occur. By familiarizing yourself with these scams, you can better protect yourself and have a more enjoyable and stress-free trip. In this guide, we will discuss some common scams in Galápagos that you should be aware of:

Unauthorized Tour Operators:

One of the most prevalent scams in Galápagos involves unauthorized tour operators. These operators may approach you on the street, offering tours or activities at significantly lower prices compared to reputable agencies. However, they may not have the necessary permits, qualified guides, or adequate safety measures in place. To avoid falling victim to this scam, always book your tours and activities through reputable and licensed operators. Do thorough research, read reviews, and ask for recommendations from trusted sources.

Fake or Counterfeit Goods:

Like many tourist destinations, Galápagos has its fair share of vendors selling souvenirs and goods. However, some vendors may try to sell fake or counterfeit items, such as handicrafts, artwork, or branded merchandise. Be cautious when making purchases and ensure you're buying from reliable sources. Authentic items may be pricier, but they are often of higher quality and support local artisans and businesses. Verify the authenticity of any high-value purchases, such as jewelry or artwork, and consider shopping at reputable stores or markets recommended by locals or trusted guides.

Taxi Overcharging:

Taxi drivers in Galápagos, as in many other places, may attempt to overcharge unsuspecting tourists. They may refuse to use the meter or negotiate a fixed fare that is significantly higher than the standard rate. To avoid this scam, familiarize yourself with the average taxi fares beforehand or inquire about the approximate cost of your journey from your accommodation or a local authority. Use licensed taxis whenever possible, and if you feel you're being overcharged, negotiate or seek an alternative mode of transportation.

Currency Exchange Scams:

It's advisable to exchange your currency at authorized exchange offices or banks to avoid falling victim to currency exchange scams. Some individuals may approach tourists on the street offering attractive exchange rates, but they may use sleight of hand or other tricks to shortchange you. Use reputable exchange facilities or withdraw money from ATMs located in well-known establishments. Keep an eye on your transactions and count your money carefully before leaving the exchange office or ATM.

Fake Park Permits:

The Galápagos National Park requires visitors to obtain permits to enter certain areas and participate in specific activities. Scammers may try to sell fake permits or claim that a permit is required when it's not. To avoid this scam, always purchase your park permits through authorized channels, such as official park offices or reputable travel agencies. Verify the authenticity of the permit, and ensure it is valid for the specific activities you plan to engage in.

Pickpocketing and Bag Snatching:

While not exclusive to Galápagos, pickpocketing and bag snatching can occur in crowded areas or tourist hotspots. It's important to take precautions to protect your belongings. Keep your valuables secure and close to your body, preferably in a bag that can be worn across your chest. Avoid displaying expensive jewelry or electronics that may attract unwanted attention. Be cautious in crowded areas, such as markets or public transportation, and be aware of your surroundings.

Time-Share and Vacation Club Scams:

In popular tourist destinations like Galápagos, you may encounter individuals offering free gifts or discounted tours in exchange for attending a timeshare or vacation club presentation. These presentations can be high-pressure sales tactics that may not deliver on their promises. If you're not interested, politely decline the offer and avoid providing personal information or signing any contracts without thoroughly understanding the terms and conditions.

What to do if in case of Emergency

In any travel destination, including Galápagos, it's important to be prepared for unexpected emergencies. While Galápagos is generally a safe place to visit, accidents, illnesses, or other emergencies can happen. Knowing what to do in case of an emergency can help you stay calm, take appropriate actions, and ensure your safety. In this guide, we will provide comprehensive information on what to do if you find yourself in an emergency situation in Galápagos.

Stay Calm and Assess the Situation:

The first and most crucial step in any emergency is to stay calm and assess the situation. Panicking can hinder your ability to think clearly and make rational decisions. Take a few deep breaths, try to remain composed, and quickly evaluate the severity of the emergency. Determine whether it requires immediate action or if it can be managed with appropriate measures.

Seek Immediate Medical Attention:

If you or someone around you requires urgent medical assistance, seek immediate medical attention. Galápagos has medical facilities and clinics available, especially in more populated areas such as Puerto Ayora and Puerto Baquerizo Moreno. Contact the local emergency services or your accommodation's front desk for guidance on the nearest medical facility. In case of a life-threatening emergency, dial the emergency hotline (911) or the local emergency number provided in the area.

Contact Your Embassy or Consulate:

In case of a significant emergency, it's advisable to contact your embassy or consulate. They can provide you with essential assistance, such as guidance, consular services, and information about local resources. Make sure to have your embassy's contact details, including phone numbers and addresses, readily available. It's a good practice to register your trip with your embassy or consulate before traveling to Galápagos, as it can help them reach you in case of an emergency.

Follow Local Authorities' Instructions:

In the event of a natural disaster, civil unrest, or any situation requiring evacuation or safety measures, it's important to follow the instructions provided by local authorities. Stay tuned to local news, radio broadcasts, or official announcements for updates and guidance. Familiarize yourself with the emergency evacuation procedures of your accommodation and be prepared to follow them if necessary.

Contact Your Travel Insurance Provider:

If you have travel insurance, contact your insurance provider as soon as possible to report the emergency and seek guidance on the coverage and claims process. They can provide assistance with medical expenses, emergency medical evacuation, trip interruption, or other benefits outlined in your policy. Keep your travel insurance policy details and emergency contact numbers accessible during your trip.

Inform Family and Friends:

It's important to keep your family and friends informed about your situation, especially in case of an emergency. Reach out to your loved ones and update them on the situation, your location, and any necessary actions you have taken. This can provide them with peace of mind and ensure that they are aware of your well-being.

Follow Safety and Security Guidelines:

Galápagos, like any other destination, has its own safety and security guidelines. Familiarize yourself with these guidelines before your trip and adhere to them during your stay. Respect local laws, customs, and traditions. Avoid unsafe areas, excessive alcohol consumption, and late-night wandering alone in unfamiliar or isolated places. By taking basic safety precautions, you can minimize the risk of emergencies and maintain your well-being.

Maintain Important Documents and Emergency Information:

It's crucial to have copies of essential documents such as your passport, identification, travel insurance policy, and emergency contact numbers. Keep these copies in a safe place separate from the originals. Additionally, save emergency contact numbers in your phone and write them down on a physical note in case your phone is lost or runs out of battery.

Be Prepared with a First Aid Kit:

Carrying a basic first aid kit is always a wise idea when traveling. Include items such as bandages, antiseptic wipes, pain relievers, insect repellent, sunscreen, and any necessary prescription medications. This can help you manage minor injuries or illnesses until you can seek professional medical attention.

Stay Informed and Exercise Caution:

Stay informed about the local conditions, weather updates, and any potential risks or hazards in Galápagos. Pay attention to travel advisories and follow the guidance provided by trusted sources such as your embassy, local authorities, or reputable travel websites. Be cautious when engaging in adventurous activities or exploring remote areas, and ensure you have proper safety equipment and trained guides if needed.

Travel Protection Insurance

Travel Protection Insurance, also known as travel insurance, is a type of insurance coverage designed to protect travelers from unforeseen events and financial losses that may occur before or during their trip. It provides a safety net and peace of mind by offering various benefits and coverage options tailored to meet the specific needs of travelers. In this chapter, I will explore travel protection insurance in detail, including its importance, key coverage areas, and tips for selecting the right policy.

Importance of Travel Protection Insurance:

Traveling involves inherent risks, and unforeseen events can disrupt even the most carefully planned trips. Travel protection insurance serves as a financial safeguard, providing coverage for various contingencies that can arise before or during your trip. It offers assistance and reimbursement for unexpected expenses, medical emergencies, trip cancellations or interruptions, lost baggage, and other mishaps. By having travel protection insurance, you can mitigate potential financial losses and ensure a smoother travel experience.

Coverage Areas:

Travel protection insurance typically offers coverage in the following areas:

a. **Trip Cancellation and Interruption**: This coverage reimburses non-refundable trip expenses if you need to cancel or cut short your trip due to covered reasons, such as illness, injury, or unforeseen events like natural disasters or terrorist attacks.

b. **Medical Expenses and Emergency Medical Evacuation**: Travel insurance provides coverage for medical expenses incurred while traveling, including hospital stays, doctor visits, and medications. It may also cover emergency medical evacuation, which is crucial if you require transportation to a medical facility or your home country for specialized treatment.

c. **Baggage and Personal Belongings**: This coverage protects against lost, stolen, or damaged luggage and personal belongings during your trip. It provides reimbursement for the cost of replacing essential items, such as clothing, toiletries, and electronic devices.

d. **Travel Delay and Missed Connections**: If your trip is delayed due to covered reasons beyond your control, travel insurance can reimburse you for additional expenses, such as accommodation, meals, and transportation. It may also cover missed connections resulting from covered events.

e. **Emergency Assistance Services**: Many travel insurance policies offer 24/7 emergency assistance services, providing access to a helpline for medical emergencies, travel advice, legal assistance, language interpretation, and other support services.

Types of Travel Protection Insurance:

There are different types of travel protection insurance policies available to cater to various travel needs. Here are some common types:

a. **Single-Trip Insurance**: This type of insurance covers a single trip, typically for a specified duration. It is ideal for travelers who plan occasional trips throughout the year.

b. **Multi-Trip Insuran**ce: Multi-trip insurance, also known as annual travel insurance, provides coverage for multiple trips within a specified time frame, usually one year. It offers convenience and cost-effectiveness for frequent travelers.

c. **Group Insurance**: Group travel insurance is designed for groups traveling together, such as families, friends, or corporate teams. It provides coverage for the entire group under a single policy.

d. **Adventure Sports Insurance**: If you plan to engage in adventure sports or activities during your trip, it's important to consider specialized insurance that covers these activities, as they may involve higher risks.

e. **Medical Insurance**: Medical travel insurance focuses primarily on providing coverage for medical emergencies and related expenses. It is especially relevant for travelers with pre-existing medical conditions or those seeking specific medical treatments abroad.

Factors to Consider When Choosing a Policy:

When selecting a travel protection insurance policy, consider the following factors:

a. **Coverage Limits**: Review the coverage limits and ensure they are sufficient to cover your potential expenses, including medical costs, trip expenses, and personal belongings.

b. **Deductibles**: Check the deductible amount, which is the portion of the claim you are responsible for paying out of pocket. A higher deductible may result in lower premiums but could increase your out-of-pocket expenses in case of a claim.

c. **Exclusions and Limitations**: Carefully read the policy to understand exclusions and limitations, as certain circumstances or activities may not be covered. Pay attention to pre-existing conditions, adventure sports, or high-value items that may require additional coverage.

d. **Policy Duration:** Ensure the policy covers the entire duration of your trip, including any pre- or post-trip activities.

e. **Provider Reputation:** Choose a reputable insurance provider with a track record of excellent customer service and timely claims processing.

Additional Tips and Considerations:

Here are some additional tips to make the most of your travel protection insurance:

a. **Read the Policy Documentation**: Familiarize yourself with the policy terms and conditions, including the claims process, required documentation, and any time limitations for filing claims.

b. **Keep Copies of Important Documents**: Make copies of your travel insurance policy, passport, visas, and other important documents. Keep one set with you and leave another set with a trusted family member or friend.

c. **Contact the Insurance Provider**: In case of an emergency or a potential claim, contact your insurance provider as soon as possible to initiate the claims process and seek guidance on the necessary steps to take.

d. **Understand Pre-Existing Conditions**: If you have pre-existing medical conditions, carefully review the policy's coverage for these conditions and any additional requirements or exclusions that may apply.

e. **Maintain Documentation**: Keep all receipts, medical records, police reports, and any other relevant documentation that may be required to support your claim.

f. **Travel Responsibly**: While travel insurance provides financial protection, it is essential to travel responsibly and take necessary precautions to ensure your safety and well-being

Where to Stay in Galápagos?

When planning a trip to Galápagos, one of the most important considerations is where to stay. The archipelago offers a range of accommodation options to suit different budgets, preferences, and travel styles. Whether you prefer luxury resorts, boutique hotels, eco-lodges, or budget-friendly hostels, Galápagos has something to offer for every traveler.

In this chapter, I will explore the different areas and types of accommodations available in Galápagos, helping you make an informed decision for your stay.

Choosing the Right Location:

Galápagos consists of several islands, and each island offers unique attractions and experiences. Understanding the characteristics of different areas can help you decide where to stay based on your interests and activities. Here are some popular islands and their highlights:

a. **Santa Cruz Island**: This is the most populated and central island in Galápagos, making it a convenient base for exploring the archipelago. Santa Cruz offers a variety of accommodations, restaurants, and shops. It is also home to the Charles Darwin Research Station, where you can learn about the conservation efforts and see giant tortoises.

b. **Isabela Island**: Known for its stunning landscapes and active volcanoes, Isabela Island offers a more laid-back and remote experience. It is ideal for nature lovers, offering opportunities for hiking, snorkeling, and wildlife encounters, including penguins and marine iguanas.

c. **San Cristóbal Island**: San Cristóbal is the easternmost island in Galápagos and offers a mix of beautiful beaches, wildlife viewing, and cultural experiences. It is a popular destination for surfing, snorkeling, and visiting the Interpretation Center to learn about the islands' history and ecosystems.

d. **Floreana Island:** For those seeking a tranquil and secluded experience, Floreana Island is an excellent choice. It is known for its pristine beaches, snorkeling spots, and the famous Post Office Bay, where you can participate in a unique postal tradition.

e. **Baltra Island**: Baltra Island is home to the main airport in Galápagos, making it a convenient arrival point. While it doesn't offer many accommodation options, staying here can be a practical choice for those with limited time or planning to join a cruise.

Types of Accommodations:

Galápagos offers a diverse range of accommodations, catering to different budgets and preferences. Here are some common types of accommodations available:

a. **Luxury Resorts:** If you're looking for upscale amenities, personalized services, and stunning locations, luxury resorts in Galápagos won't disappoint. These resorts often offer lavish accommodations, fine dining options, spa facilities, and access to private beaches.

b. **Boutique Hotels**: Galápagos is dotted with charming boutique hotels that provide a unique and intimate experience. These smaller, independently-owned properties often have stylish decor, personalized service, and a cozy ambiance.

c. **Eco-Lodges**: For eco-conscious travelers, Galápagos offers various eco-lodges that prioritize sustainability and environmental conservation. These accommodations blend harmoniously with the natural surroundings, providing a close-to-nature experience without compromising comfort.

d. **Hostels**: Budget-friendly travelers will find a selection of hostels and guesthouses in Galápagos. These options offer shared or private rooms, communal spaces, and a social atmosphere, making them ideal for backpackers or those seeking affordable accommodations.

e. **Liveaboard Cruises:** Another unique accommodation option in Galápagos is to stay on a liveaboard cruise. These cruises offer the opportunity to explore multiple islands, enjoy guided excursions, and experience the archipelago's diverse marine life. Live aboard cruises range from budget to luxury, providing different levels of comfort and amenities.

Considerations for Choosing Accommodations:

When selecting accommodations in Galápagos, consider the following factors to ensure a comfortable and enjoyable stay:

a. **Proximity to Attractions**: Determine which activities and attractions are on your must-visit list and choose accommodations that offer convenient access to those places. This will save you time and transportation costs.

b. **Amenities and Services**: Assess the facilities and services provided by the accommodations, such as Wi-Fi, air conditioning, swimming pools, on-site restaurants, tour arrangements, and airport transfers. Prioritize the amenities that are important to you.

c. **Reviews and Ratings**: Read reviews and ratings from previous guests to get insights into the quality of service, cleanliness, and overall guest experience. Websites like TripAdvisor and Booking.com can provide valuable feedback from fellow travelers.

d. **Price and Value**: Set a budget for your accommodations and compare prices to ensure you're getting the best value for your money. Consider the location, facilities, and services offered to determine if the price aligns with your expectations.

e. **Safety and Security**: Look for accommodations that prioritize guest safety and provide necessary security measures. Check if the property has 24-hour front desk service, secure locks, and safety deposit boxes.

Booking in Advance:

Due to the popularity of Galápagos as a travel destination, it is advisable to book accommodations in advance, especially during peak seasons. By securing your accommodations ahead of time, you can ensure availability and have a wider range of options to choose from.

Local Regulations and Sustainability:

When choosing accommodations in Galápagos, consider establishments that adhere to local regulations and sustainability practices. Look for accommodations that support local communities, minimize their environmental impact, and promote responsible tourism.

This page was left blank intentionally

Resources for Solo Travelers

Solo travel can be an incredibly rewarding and enriching experience. It allows you to explore new destinations at your own pace, immerse yourself in different cultures, and gain a sense of independence and self-discovery. If you're planning a solo adventure, it's important to have the right resources and information to ensure a safe and enjoyable trip. In this guide, we will explore various resources that can be valuable for solo travelers, helping you navigate your journey with confidence.

Online Travel Communities:

Online travel communities are a great resource for solo travelers. These platforms provide a space for connecting with fellow travelers, sharing experiences, and seeking advice. Websites like Lonely Planet's Thorn Tree, TripAdvisor forums, and Reddit's r/solotravel are popular platforms where you can find information, ask questions, and receive recommendations from experienced solo travelers.

Travel Blogs and Websites:

Travel blogs and websites are an excellent source of inspiration and practical information for solo travelers. Many seasoned travelers share their experiences, tips, and itineraries on their blogs, providing valuable insights into various destinations. Websites like Nomadic Matt, The Blonde Abroad, and Adventurous Kate are popular choices for solo travel content.

Guidebooks:

Guidebooks are a reliable resource for solo travelers, providing comprehensive information about destinations, attractions, accommodations, and transportation options. Popular guidebook series like Lonely Planet, Rick Steves, and Fodor's offer detailed insights into different countries and cities, along with maps and practical tips for navigating your way around.

Travel Apps:

Travel apps have become indispensable tools for solo travelers. They offer a range of features to enhance your travel experience, including maps, language translation, currency conversion, and accommodation bookings. Apps like Google Maps, Duolingo, XE Currency, and Airbnb are must-haves for solo travelers, providing convenience and accessibility on the go.

Safety Resources:

Safety is a top concern for solo travelers, and there are resources available to help ensure your well-being during your journey. Websites like the U.S. Department of State's Travel Advisory, the UK Foreign and Commonwealth Office, and the Australian Government's Smart Traveller provide up-to-date information on travel warnings, safety tips, and country-specific advice.

Travel Insurance:

Travel insurance is essential for any traveler, but particularly for solo travelers. It provides financial protection in case of emergencies, medical expenses, trip cancellations, or lost belongings. Research and compare different travel insurance providers to find a policy that suits your needs and covers the activities you plan to engage in during your solo trip.

Local Tourism Websites:

When traveling solo, it's beneficial to consult the official tourism websites of the destinations you plan to visit. These websites provide information on attractions, local events, transportation options, and safety guidelines specific to the region. They can also be a useful resource for finding reliable tour operators, local guides, and recommended accommodations.

Solo Travel Tours and Groups:

If you prefer the companionship of like-minded travelers, joining solo travel tours or groups can be a fantastic option. Several tour operators specialize in organizing trips for solo travelers, providing the opportunity to explore destinations with a group while still maintaining the independence of solo travel. Websites like G Adventures and Intrepid Travel offer a wide range of solo travel tour options.

Local Contacts and Networking:

Building local contacts can enhance your solo travel experience by providing insider tips, local recommendations, and even the opportunity to meet up with locals or fellow travelers. Online platforms like Couchsurfing, Meetup, and various travel-specific Facebook groups allow you to connect with locals and other travelers in the destinations you plan to visit.

Travel Safety Apps:

Travel safety apps are designed to provide added security and peace of mind for solo travelers. These apps offer features like real-time location tracking, emergency contact information, and SOS alerts. Popular travel safety apps include TripWhistle, bSafe, and GeoSure.

This page was left blank intentionally

15 Best Place to Stay in Galápagos for Affordable Price

When planning a trip to the Galápagos Islands, finding affordable accommodation that offers comfort, convenience, and a great location is essential. In this guide, we will explore 15 of the best places to stay in Galápagos that offer affordable prices without compromising on quality. We will discuss their features, pros and cons, as well as provide an overview of the price range to help you make an informed decision.

Hostal Galápagos:

Features: Hostal Galápagos is a budget-friendly option located in Puerto Ayora on Santa Cruz Island. It offers comfortable rooms with private bathrooms, free Wi-Fi, and a shared kitchen. The hostel also has a terrace where guests can relax and enjoy the views.

Pros: Affordable rates, convenient location, friendly staff, shared kitchen facilities.

Cons: Basic amenities, limited on-site services.

Price: Prices start at around $40 per night.

Hotel Fiesta:

Features: Hotel Fiesta is situated in Puerto Ayora and provides cozy rooms with private bathrooms, air conditioning, and free Wi-Fi. The hotel has a restaurant and bar, offering a variety of local and international dishes.

Pros: Reasonable rates, central location, on-site dining options.

Cons: Limited amenities, basic facilities.

Price: Prices start at approximately $50 per night.

Hotel Ninfa:

Features: Hotel Ninfa is a budget-friendly hotel located in Puerto Ayora. It offers comfortable rooms with private bathrooms, air conditioning, and free Wi-Fi. The hotel has a restaurant and a tour desk that can assist with booking activities and excursions.

Pros: Affordable rates, central location, helpful staff, on-site dining options.

Cons: Basic amenities, limited facilities.

Price: Prices start at around $60 per night.

Hotel Lobo de Mar:

Features: Hotel Lobo de Mar is situated in Puerto Ayora and provides comfortable rooms with private bathrooms, air conditioning, and free Wi-Fi. The hotel offers a complimentary breakfast and has a rooftop terrace with panoramic views of the town.

Pros: Affordable rates, convenient location, complimentary breakfast, rooftop terrace.

Cons: Limited amenities, basic facilities.

Price: Prices start at approximately $70 per night.

Hostal Cerro Azul:

Features: Hostal Cerro Azul is a budget-friendly accommodation located in Puerto Baquerizo Moreno on San Cristobal Island. It offers simple yet comfortable rooms with private bathrooms and free Wi-Fi. The hostel has a communal kitchen and a terrace.

Pros: Affordable rates, convenient location, communal kitchen facilities.

Cons: Basic amenities, limited on-site services.

Price: Prices start at around $40 per night.

Hotel Katarma:

Features: Hotel Katarma is situated in Puerto Baquerizo Moreno and offers comfortable rooms with private bathrooms, air conditioning, and free Wi-Fi. The hotel has a restaurant, a bar, and a terrace where guests can relax and enjoy the views.

Pros: Reasonable rates, central location, on-site dining options, terrace.

Cons: Limited amenities, basic facilities.

Price: Prices start at approximately $60 per night.

Hotel Mar Azul:

Features: Hotel Mar Azul is located in Puerto Ayora and provides comfortable rooms with private bathrooms, air conditioning, and free Wi-Fi. The hotel has a restaurant, a bar, and a garden where guests can unwind.

Pros: Affordable rates, central location, on-site dining options, garden area.

Cons: Limited amenities, basic facilities.

Price: Prices start at around $70 per night.

Hostal Gardner Galápagos:

Features: Hostal Gardner Galápagos is situated in Puerto Baquerizo Moreno and offers cozy rooms with private bathrooms, air conditioning, and free Wi-Fi. The hostel has a communal kitchen, a terrace, and a shared lounge area.

Pros: Affordable rates, convenient location, communal kitchen facilities, terrace.

Cons: Basic amenities, limited on-site services.

Price: Prices start at approximately $50 per night.

Hotel Red Booby:

Features: Hotel Red Booby is located in Puerto Ayora and provides comfortable rooms with private bathrooms, air conditioning, and free Wi-Fi. The hotel has a restaurant, a bar, and a rooftop terrace with panoramic views of the town.

Pros: Reasonable rates, central location, on-site dining options, rooftop terrace.

Cons: Limited amenities, basic facilities.

Price: Prices start at around $80 per night.

Hotel Blue Marlin:

Features: Hotel Blue Marlin is situated in Puerto Ayora and offers comfortable rooms with private bathrooms, air conditioning, and free Wi-Fi. The hotel has a restaurant, a bar, and a garden area where guests can relax.

Pros: Affordable rates, central location, on-site dining options, garden area.

Cons: Limited amenities, basic facilities.

Price: Prices start at approximately $70 per night.

Hotel Espana:

Features: Hotel Espana is located in Puerto Ayora and provides cozy rooms with private bathrooms, air conditioning, and free Wi-Fi. The hotel has a restaurant, a bar, and a terrace where guests can enjoy the views.

Pros: Affordable rates, convenient location, on-site dining options, terrace.

Cons: Limited amenities, basic facilities.

Price: Prices start at around $80 per night.

Hostal Tintorera:

Features: Hostal Tintorera is situated in Puerto Villamil on Isabela Island. It offers comfortable rooms with private bathrooms, air conditioning, and free Wi-Fi. The hostel has a shared kitchen, a terrace, and a garden area.

Pros: Affordable rates, convenient location, communal kitchen facilities, terrace.

Cons: Basic amenities, limited on-site services.

Price: Prices start at approximately $60 per night.

Hotel San Vicente Galápagos:

Features: Hotel San Vicente Galápagos is located in Puerto Ayora and provides comfortable rooms with private bathrooms, air conditioning, and free Wi-Fi. The hotel has a restaurant, a bar, and a garden area for guests to relax.

Pros: Reasonable rates, central location, on-site dining options, garden area.

Cons: Limited amenities, basic facilities.

Price: Prices start at around $70 per night.

Hostal Galápagos Morning Glory:

Features: Hostal Galápagos Morning Glory is situated in Puerto Baquerizo Moreno and offers cozy rooms with private bathrooms, air conditioning, and free Wi-Fi. The hostel has a communal kitchen, a terrace, and a shared lounge area.

Pros: Affordable rates, convenient location, communal kitchen facilities, terrace.

Cons: Basic amenities, limited on-site services.

Price: Prices start at approximately $50 per night.

Hotel Scalesia Galápagos Lodge:

Features: Hotel Scalesia Galápagos Lodge is located in Puerto Villamil on Isabela Island. It offers comfortable rooms with private bathrooms, air conditioning, and free Wi-Fi. The hotel has a restaurant, a bar, and a garden where guests can relax and enjoy the views.

Pros: Affordable rates, convenient location, on-site dining options, garden area.

Cons: Limited amenities, basic facilities.

Price: Prices start at around $120 per night.

This page was left blank intentionally

15 Best Luxuries Hotel to Stay in Galápagos

These 15 best luxury hotels in Galápagos offer a range of amenities, stunning locations, and unique experiences. Whether you're seeking secluded tranquility or convenient access to attractions, there's a luxury hotel that suits your preferences. Remember to check for seasonal rates and availability when planning your stay in Galápagos.

1. Pikaia Lodge:

Features: Pikaia Lodge is a luxurious eco-retreat located in Santa Cruz. It offers spacious rooms with panoramic views, private terraces, and modern amenities. The lodge features a gourmet restaurant, a spa, a swimming pool, and offers exclusive access to their private yacht for exploring the islands.

Pros: Exclusive access to a private yacht, stunning views, eco-friendly practices, exceptional dining options.

Cons: High-end pricing.

Price: Prices start at approximately $1,000 per night.

2. Finch Bay Galápagos Hotel:

Features: Finch Bay Galápagos Hotel is nestled in a secluded location in Puerto Ayora on Santa Cruz Island. It offers comfortable rooms, a swimming pool, a spa, and direct access to the beach. The hotel also offers a variety of eco-friendly activities and excursions.

Pros: Secluded location, beach access, eco-friendly practices, outdoor activities.

Cons: Limited on-site dining options.

Price: Prices start at around $500 per night.

3. Royal Palm Hotel Galápagos:

Features: Royal Palm Hotel Galápagos is a luxury boutique hotel located in the highlands of Santa Cruz Island. It offers spacious villas and suites, an outdoor swimming pool, a spa, and beautifully landscaped gardens. The hotel also provides access to exclusive nature trails and has its own tortoise reserve.

Pros: Tranquil location, luxurious accommodations, access to nature trails, tortoise reserve.

Cons: Limited dining options, remote location.

Price: Prices start at approximately $800 per night.

4. Pikaia Lodge Santa Cruz:

Features: Pikaia Lodge Santa Cruz is a luxurious retreat nestled in the highlands of Santa Cruz Island. It offers elegant rooms with stunning views, a swimming pool, a spa, and a gourmet restaurant. Guests can also explore the private wild giant tortoise reserve on the property.

Pros: Breathtaking views, luxurious amenities, gourmet dining, private tortoise reserve.

Cons: Expensive rates, remote location.

Price: Prices start at around $1,200 per night.

5. Iguana Crossing Boutique Hotel:

Features: Iguana Crossing Boutique Hotel is situated in Puerto Villamil on Isabela Island. It offers stylish rooms with ocean views, an outdoor swimming pool, a rooftop terrace, and a restaurant serving local and international cuisine. The hotel provides easy access to the nearby Flamingo Lagoon and Sierra Negra Volcano.

Pros: Oceanfront location, rooftop terrace, proximity to natural attractions.

Cons: Limited on-site facilities, remote location.

Price: Prices start at approximately $400 per night.

6. Hotel Solymar Galápagos:

Features: Hotel Solymar Galápagos is located in Puerto Ayora on Santa Cruz Island. It offers comfortable rooms with ocean views, an outdoor swimming pool, a restaurant, and direct access to the beach. The hotel also organizes snorkeling and diving excursions for guests.

Pros: Beachfront location, swimming pool, snorkeling and diving opportunities.

Cons: Limited on-site facilities, can be crowded during peak seasons.

Price: Prices start at around $400 per night.

7. Galápagos Safari Camp:

Features: Galápagos Safari Camp is a unique luxury tented camp located in the highlands of Santa Cruz Island. It offers spacious tented suites with stunning views, a swimming pool, a restaurant, and a variety of outdoor activities such as hiking, biking, and horseback riding.

Pros: Unique tented accommodations, panoramic views, outdoor activities.

Cons: Remote location, limited dining options.

Price: Prices start at approximately $900 per night.

8. The Angermeyer Waterfront Inn:

Features: The Angermeyer Waterfront Inn is situated in Puerto Ayora on Santa Cruz Island. It offers charming rooms with a waterfront view, a swimming pool, a restaurant, and a bar. The inn is located within walking distance of popular attractions and has a private dock.

Pros: Waterfront location, swimming pool, convenient access to attractions.

Cons: Limited on-site facilities, can be noisy due to proximity to the town.

Price: Prices start at around $300 per night.

9. Red Mangrove Aventura Lodge:

Features: Red Mangrove Aventura Lodge is located in Puerto Ayora on Santa Cruz Island. It offers comfortable rooms, a swimming pool, a restaurant, and a lounge bar. The lodge provides access to various land and water-based activities, including snorkeling and kayaking.

Pros: Central location, swimming pool, access to activities.

Cons: Basic amenities, can be crowded during peak seasons.

Price: Prices start at approximately $300 per night.

10. Golden Bay Hotel & Spa:

Features: Golden Bay Hotel & Spa is situated in Puerto Baquerizo Moreno on San Cristobal Island. It offers modern rooms with ocean views, an outdoor swimming pool, a spa, and a restaurant serving international and local cuisine. The hotel also offers easy access to nearby beaches and attractions.

Pros: Ocean views, swimming pool, spa facilities, proximity to attractions.

Cons: Limited dining options, can be noisy due to proximity to the town.

Price: Prices start at around $400 per night.

11. Hotel Fiesta:

Features: Hotel Fiesta is located in Puerto Ayora on Santa Cruz Island. It offers comfortable rooms, a swimming pool, a restaurant, and a bar. The hotel provides a central location, making it convenient for exploring the town and its attractions.

Pros: Central location, swimming pool, affordable rates.

Cons: Basic amenities, can be noisy due to proximity to the town.

Price: Prices start at approximately $200 per night.

12. Hotel Casa Natura Galápagos:

Features: Hotel Casa Natura Galápagos is situated in Puerto Ayora on Santa Cruz Island. It offers cozy rooms, a swimming pool, a restaurant, and a bar. The hotel also has a garden area and provides easy access to nearby attractions and restaurants.

Pros: Cozy accommodations, swimming pool, garden area, proximity to attractions.

Cons: Limited on-site facilities, can be noisy during peak seasons.

Price: Prices start at around $200 per night.

13. Hotel Silberstein:

Features: Hotel Silberstein is located in Puerto Ayora on Santa Cruz Island. It offers comfortable rooms, a swimming pool, a restaurant, and a bar. The hotel is situated near the waterfront and provides easy access to local shops and restaurants.

Pros: Waterfront location, swimming pool, proximity to shops and restaurants.

Cons: Basic amenities, limited on-site facilities.

Price: Prices start at approximately $200 per night.

14. Hotel Albemarle:

Features: Hotel Albemarle is situated in Puerto Villamil on Isabela Island. It offers comfortable rooms, a swimming pool, a restaurant, and a bar. The hotel provides easy access to the beach and is within walking distance of local attractions and restaurants.

Pros: Beach access, swimming pool, proximity to attractions.

Cons: Basic amenities, limited dining options.

Price: Prices start at around $200 per night.

15. Hotel Sol y Mar:

Features: Hotel Sol y Mar is located in Puerto Ayora on Santa Cruz Island. It offers comfortable rooms, a swimming pool, a restaurant, and a bar. The hotel provides a central location, making it convenient for exploring the town and its attractions.

Pros: Central location, swimming pool, affordable rates.

Cons: Basic amenities, can be noisy due to proximity to the town.

Price: Prices start at approximately $150 per night.

10 Most Delicious Food You Should Try in Galápagos

When visiting Galápagos, not only will you be captivated by its natural beauty and wildlife, but you'll also have the opportunity to indulge in a variety of delicious local cuisine. The Galápagos Islands offer a unique culinary experience that combines fresh seafood, local produce, and traditional Ecuadorian flavors. Here are 10 mouthwatering dishes that you must try during your visit to Galápagos:

Ceviche:

Ceviche is a popular dish in Galápagos, and it consists of fresh seafood, typically fish or shrimp, marinated in lime juice and mixed with onions, tomatoes, cilantro, and other seasonings. The acidity of the lime juice "cooks" the seafood, resulting in a refreshing and flavorful dish. Ceviche is often served as an appetizer or a light meal. The cost per plate ranges from $10 to $15.

Pros: Fresh and tangy flavors, highlights the quality of Galápagos seafood.

Cons: May not be suitable for those with a sensitivity to raw seafood.

Encocado de Pescado:

Encocado de Pescado is a delicious fish stew prepared with coconut milk, onions, peppers, and spices. The fish is cooked in the flavorful coconut broth until tender and served with rice and plantains. The dish has a creamy texture and a rich, tropical taste. The cost per plate ranges from $15 to $20.

Pros: Creamy and flavorful, a perfect combination of fish and coconut.

Cons: May not be suitable for those with a nut allergy.

Llapingachos:

Llapingachos are traditional Ecuadorian potato cakes that are popular throughout the country, including Galápagos. They are made with mashed potatoes, cheese, and onions, and then cooked on a griddle until golden brown. Llapingachos are typically served as a side dish with grilled meats or fried eggs. The cost per plate ranges from $5 to $8.

Pros: Crispy on the outside, soft and cheesy on the inside.

Cons: Can be heavy and filling.

Encebollado:

Encebollado is a hearty fish soup that is often considered Ecuador's national dish. It is made with fresh tuna, onions, tomatoes, yuca (cassava), and spices. The soup has a rich and flavorful broth, and it is usually served with corn tortillas or plantain chips. Encebollado is a popular lunchtime meal among locals. The cost per bowl ranges from $10 to $15.

Pros: Flavorful and comforting, showcases the local seafood.

Cons: May have a strong fish aroma.

Seco de Pollo:

Seco de Pollo is a traditional Ecuadorian chicken stew that is slow-cooked with onions, peppers, garlic, cumin, and other spices. The dish has a thick and savory sauce, and it is typically served with rice, avocado slices, and a side of salad. The cost per plate ranges from $10 to $15.

Pros: Tender and flavorful chicken, comforting and filling.

Cons: Can be heavy and may not suit those with dietary restrictions.

Bolón de Verde:

Bolón de Verde is a popular Ecuadorian breakfast or snack item. It is made from mashed green plantains mixed with cheese and formed into a ball, which is then fried until crispy. Bolón de Verde is often served with eggs, cheese, and avocado. The cost per plate ranges from $5 to $8.

Pros: Crispy and flavorful, a great combination of textures.

Cons: Can be greasy.

Pescado a la Plancha:

Pescado a la Plancha is a simple yet delicious dish that showcases the freshness of Galápagos fish. The fish is seasoned with salt, pepper, and herbs, and then grilled or pan-fried until perfectly cooked. It is typically served with rice, plantains, and a side of salad. The cost per plate ranges from $15 to $20.

Pros: Fresh and light, allows the natural flavors of the fish to shine.

Cons: Limited seasoning, may require additional condiments for flavor.

Empanadas:

Empanadas are a popular snack in Galápagos and throughout Ecuador. They are stuffed pastries filled with various ingredients, such as cheese, meat, seafood, or vegetables. Empanadas are then baked or fried until golden and crispy. They are perfect for a quick and tasty bite on the go. The cost per empanada ranges from $2 to $5.

Pros: Portable and versatile, available with different fillings.

Cons: Can be greasy depending on the cooking method.

Churrasco:

Churrasco is a grilled beef dish that is commonly found in Ecuador. It consists of tender beef steak seasoned with salt, pepper, and garlic, and then grilled to perfection. Churrasco is typically served with rice, beans, fried plantains, and a side salad. The cost per plate ranges from $15 to $25.

Pros: Juicy and flavorful beef, satisfying and filling.

Cons: May not be suitable for vegetarians or those with dietary restrictions.

Tigrillo:

Tigrillo is a traditional Ecuadorian breakfast dish made from mashed green plantains mixed with cheese, eggs, and sometimes pork or chorizo. The mixture is cooked until it forms a thick and creamy consistency. Tigrillo is typically served with coffee, bread, and a side of avocado. The cost per plate ranges from $5 to $8.

Pros: Creamy and flavorful, a unique breakfast experience.

Cons: Can be heavy for some people in the morning.

Conclusion

As I reflect on my unforgettable vacation in Galápagos, I can't help but feel overwhelmed with gratitude for the incredible experiences and memories I have made during my time on these enchanted islands. From the moment I set foot on this unique archipelago, I knew I was in for an extraordinary adventure unlike any other.

My journey began with a warm welcome to Galápagos, where I was immediately captivated by the natural beauty that surrounded me. The pristine beaches, turquoise waters, and dramatic landscapes were a sight to behold. I spent my days exploring the diverse ecosystems, hiking through volcanic terrain, and snorkeling in crystal-clear waters teeming with vibrant marine life. Every moment was a reminder of the extraordinary biodiversity that Galápagos is renowned for.

One of the highlights of my trip was encountering the incredible wildlife that calls Galápagos home. I had the privilege of observing giant tortoises in their natural habitat, playful sea lions basking in the sun, and magnificent frigatebirds soaring through the sky. It was a humbling experience to witness the harmony between humans and animals in this pristine environment, and it served as a reminder of the importance of conservation efforts to preserve this delicate ecosystem.

The culinary delights of Galápagos also left a lasting impression on me. From savoring the freshest seafood in mouthwatering ceviche to indulging in traditional Ecuadorian dishes like encocado de pescado and llapingachos, my taste buds were constantly treated to a symphony of flavors. Each meal was a culinary journey that celebrated the local ingredients and traditions, further enhancing my overall experience in Galápagos.

Beyond the natural wonders and gastronomic delights, the people of Galápagos played a significant role in making my vacation truly memorable. The warmth and hospitality of the locals were evident in every interaction, from the guides who shared their extensive knowledge and passion for the islands to the locals who welcomed me with open arms. Their genuine kindness and willingness to share their culture and stories added a personal touch to my journey, making me feel like a part of the Galápagos community.

Throughout my stay, I also had the opportunity to explore the various islands that make up the Galápagos archipelago. Each island had its unique charm and offerings, from the dramatic landscapes of Isabela Island to the stunning wildlife encounters on Santa Cruz Island. The diversity of experiences within Galápagos ensured that every day was filled with new discoveries and adventures.

As my vacation in Galápagos came to a close, I couldn't help but feel a sense of awe and gratitude for the transformative experience I had. The pristine beauty of the islands, the awe-inspiring wildlife encounters, the delectable cuisine, and the warm hospitality of the people all contributed to a truly exceptional journey. Galápagos had not only provided me with incredible memories but also a deep appreciation for the delicate balance of nature and the importance of conservation efforts.

Leaving Galápagos was bittersweet, as I bid farewell to the breathtaking landscapes, the gentle ocean breezes, and the incredible wildlife that had become a part of my daily life. However, I left with a renewed commitment to preserve and protect this unique ecosystem for future generations to enjoy.

My vacation in Galápagos was a once-in-a-lifetime experience that exceeded all expectations. It was a journey that awakened my sense of wonder, instilled in me a deep respect for nature, and left an indelible mark on my soul. Galápagos will forever hold a special place in my heart, and I am grateful for the opportunity to have experienced its magic and beauty firsthand. Until we meet again, Galápagos, I carry with me the memories of our time together and the lessons learned from this extraordinary destination.

Printed in Great Britain
by Amazon